ENDORSEMENTS

Seemingly simple and yet simultaneously profound, this treatise on God's holy love is informed by the author's extensive knowledge of biblical languages and culture. Babbitt writes with creative language and rich imagery, helping the reader to comprehend that which seems incomprehensible. While impossible to fully plumb the depths of God's love, Love Never Fails *calls us to intimately encounter God's intense and complete love for us, so that our love toward God and toward others can be wholly formed by that knowledge and experience.*

Rev. Jonathan K. Twitchell
Author, Presence: A Pastor's Guide to Funerals

I liked Steve Babbitt's writing when I was one of his college professors. After reading Love Never Fails, *I like it even more. It's witty, deep and challenging. It will make you want to receive this Love immediately, and then show it to the world.*

Dean Nelson, Ph.D.
Journalism Program Director, Point Loma Nazarene University
Author, God Hides in Plain Sight: How to See the Sacred in a Chaotic World, *and* Talk To Me: How To Ask Better Questions, Get Better Answers, and Interview Anyone Like A Pro

---

Pastors today are bombarded by congregants who suffer from scores of spiritual, mental, emotional, and physical ailments. At times, their problems seem insurmountable. Life can appear to be bleak and foreboding. Congregants turn to their pastors for answers... for **The Answer**... *to their problems. The compilation of all of these difficulties, and the desire to help those in their flock who suffer from them, can exert incredible pressure on any one pastor.*

Steve Babbitt, Pastor of the Spring Valley Community Church, has recognized that **The Answer** *to today's complex problems is a simple one. He also knows that this simple answer is not always an easy one. It's one that demands the destruction of self-centeredness, and one that requires a belief in, and a conscious contact with, God. He knows too that neither he, nor we, are here to* *solve these problems. What we are 'here' for is to harvest and distribute God's "Holy Love." God is the solution to all problems, because God is Love.*

Pastor Babbitt's concepts made me pause and reflect on God's 'commandments' from a perspective I hadn't previously considered in such a light. From Genesis, God first commands us to be **fruitful** *(which brings forth many connotations). Next, Christ commands that we* **Love God with our whole being, and to love our neighbor as our-self**. *And finally, Christ commands His followers to* **love one another, as I have loved you.** *Congregants may not initially realize that the solution to their worldly difficulties are contained within these commands, but if followed, they will soon see that their worldly difficulties will diminish into obscurity. God's Holy Love, internalized, is the answer.*

Christ calls us out of the world in order that we may be **changed.** *Christ then sends us back into the world with the Holy mandate to be* **fruitful** *and share* **The Good News of God's Holy Love.** *The Holy premise of the Good News is the topic of Pastor Steve Babbitt's book:* **Love, Holy Love. The Love that Never Fails.**

H. Spencer O'Neal
Doctor in Addictive Disorders
Licensed Educational Psychologist
Certified Alcohol & Drug Counselor
Board Certified Professional Christian Counselor
Author, Spirituality in Addictions Counseling: A Clinician's Guide

---

Don't read this book . . . quickly. You can't hurry love. Love is not cursory or shallow. Love is not perfunctory. It is not hasty or careless. Love is not slipshod or slapdash. We know love; the definitions, the canon of illustrations, and the sermons are asphalt on our hearts and minds. Read this book slowly, unhurriedly. Steve's book is best served with coffee over a dozen quiet mornings.

Dennis Leggett, Ed.D.
Child Welfare Services, County of San Diego
Author, The Saint Louise de Merillac Devotional for Social Workers

---

"After reading Love Never Fails *by Steve Babbitt, I was overwhelmed. POWERFUL and LIFE-CHANGING are the best words that I can use to describe it. This text spoke to me in so many ways – I love the down-to-earth language, the meaningful metaphors and examples, and the way the author has woven scripture throughout the text to keep us focused on the WORD. God's love for us is something that we hear about regularly in church or read about in the Bible,*

but Love Never Fails *made it come alive for me. This book reminded me how short I fall and where I need to be going, and will continue to speak to me every time I re-read it.*

Dr. Kathy Gloyd
Founder, ElevateDVM

Love Never Fails *is a quick, convicting, yet encouraging read. Steve writes with clarity, passion and compassion about what I know to be his life goal - to grow in his understanding of God's love for him, and to be a free flowing channel of that love to his family, his congregation, his community and yes, even his enemies. Having known Steve for over 20 years as a fellow minister, but more importantly as a dear friend, there are few people I know that better exemplify the unfailing love of Jesus Christ. So pour yourself a cup of coffee, pull up a chair and dive into Love Never Fails. You won't be disappointed!*

Rev. Scott Archer
Senior Pastor, La Mesa Central Congregational Church, La Mesa, CA

Love Never Fails *is a holy work of love. Steve Babbitt shares a depth of love that is genuine, steadfast in sharing spiritual truth, and calls all to know and experience a love that never fails, to embrace a Holy Love. I encourage you to read it as he dared to write it, with an openness to "dig down deep and wrestle" with a subject that is foreign to all of us.*

Jim Johnson, Ed.D.
Professor, Consultant, Life Mentor and Coach

"Human Love is a copy of the original—sometimes convincing but ultimately a forgery of—the great love that is God," so writes Pastor Steve Babbitt. Throughout this work, Steve continually draws his reader back to the central point of God's Holy Love. This book serves as a reminder that while my human love is full of limitations, God's Holy Love is without limits. Steve invites his readers into that life of Holy Love in order, as his title states, to Love Wholly. For the better part of 25 years I have known Steve and been witness to his willingness to give love, receive love, and grow in love throughout his journey as a husband, father, pastor and friend. Anyone (i.e. all of us) who needs to be reminded of God's rich love and the implications that embracing this Holy Love has on your life must read this book.

Michael Hoggatt, Ph.D.
Learning Disabilities Instructor, Saddleback College
Author, Moving to the Manger: A Journey from Exclusion to Inclusion

I have written 7 books, all in the engineering genre, and that is because, as my friends will attest, I hate lazy logic, cluttered calculations and imprecise implications. By page 21 of this marvelous book I realized more deeply and more clearly why I've always like conversations with its author, Steve Babbitt. Razor sharp insights based on crystal clear logic carefully calculated to force you to stop and assess your thinking, your assumptions, your perspective. The gift given to, and nurtured by, Steve comes through in the written word as reliably as it does in those conversations I love. Maybe even better because of the internal dialogue it fosters about the real stuff of life. The stuff I'd just as soon put off until later like, I think, so many others. Brighten your mind and lift your spirit by enjoying this book with a cup of your favorite morning or evening beverage!

John G. Stenbeck, PMP, PMI-ACP, CSM, CSP
Speaker | Author | Entrepreneur
Enterprise Agility Expert
Three-time Amazon #1 Best Selling Author
John Maxwell Certified Coach, Trainer & Speaker
Maxwell Certified Behavioral Analysis Trainer

Steve Babbitt's book, **Love Never Fails: Knowing Holy Love So We Can Love Wholly,** *is an incredibly important work offering deep insights into the relationship between God's love and the human condition. Steve has a talent for incorporating the Bible's concepts with his knowledge of history, literature, and ancient languages. The author lands the high notions of God's transcendental love on the shores of real, human life – our marriages, our neighborhoods and our communities. Steve creatively makes use of imagination, vivid imagery, stories and practical illustrations. I recommend this book to any Christian who wishes to understand the depth of God's love, but also to any preacher seeking fresh ideas for sermons and teaching.*

Vladimir Ubeivolc, Ph.D.
President of Beginning of Life NGO | www.bol.md
Senior Pastor of Life to the World Church, Chisinau, Moldova
Author, The New Face of Human Trafficking

The Creator has blessed Steve with a creative spark unlike any other. I'd seen that spark in his music, design, and speaking, but now to see it ignite in written form is a true joy.

Love Never Fails *sends readers backpedaling to the starting line of the Christian life—the holy love of God—only to then catapult you forward on a jet-fueled jaunt through the wild wonders of God's mercy and grace. Babbitt is wise and true navigator on this journey, and all I can guarantee is that you'll end up in a place of deeper trust in God's rock-solid love.*

Rev. Ryan Murphy
Christian Author, Educator, Missionary, and Pastor
Author, All That You Can't Leave Behind *and* Winter Spring Summer Fall

Steve Babbitt invites us to consider the meaning of Love Never Fails *again. At the heart of his message is a call to deepen our knowledge of Holy Love so We Can Love Wholly. This is a resource to both clergy and laity; pastors will find this to be a useful resource for sermons on this subject matter, laity and clergy will find in this book a tool for Spiritual Formation of the body.*

Filimão M. Chambo, Ph.D.
General Superintendent, Church of the Nazarene

LoveNeverFails

Knowing Holy Love So We Can Love Wholly

MAY THE LOVE OF
OUR LORD BE WITH
YOU, NOW AND
ALWAYS!

— STEVE BABBITT

LoveNeverFails

Knowing Holy Love So We Can Love Wholly

STEVE BABBITT

*Book One of The **Fruit of the Spirit** Series*

Love Never Fails
Knowing Holy Love So We Can Love Wholly

ISBN # 978-1-7332002-0-2

Published by:
Two Tees Press
10174 Austin Drive, #1845
Spring Valley, CA 91977

Editor: Lauren Mix of LM Editing
www.LMeditingservices.com | LMeditservices@gmail.com
603-660-9090

Book/Cover Design: Tamara Parsons
Kensington Type & Graphics | www.kentype.com

DEDICATION

To Cambria, James, and John
&
To Scarlett and Griff
May your love never grow old!

TABLE OF CONTENTS

ACKNOWLEDGEMENTS

These meditations come from a series of sermons delivered at Spring Valley Community Church in the wilting hot summer of 2018. As such, I am indebted to my very generous congregation for allowing me to experiment on them. Spring Valley may be a small church, but it has colossal heart!

Bringing words originally spoken aloud to print was far more challenging than I thought it would be. I must express my deepest gratitude to Brooke Yeider, Paige O'Neal, and Lauren Mix who were thorough in their tough comments, inspired suggestions, and downright good editing! Your patient and powerful insights have brought the spoken word to life on the written page.

I would also like to express my admiration and appreciation for Caden Dougherty, who provided musical bookends for the audio version of *Love Never Fails*. I can't wait to see how the Lord uses your many gifts in the future, young man!

Finally, to my beloved wife and true companion Tammie – you already know how much your words of encouragement mean to me. Thank you for believing in me. The best is truly yet to be!

FRUIT FIRST

About The Fruit of the Spirit Series

"By their fruits you will know them." (Matthew 7.20)

How do you measure spiritual vitality? So much of what we're doing is not what God wants us to do. His desire? That we abide in Him, as branches in the vine, and that through abiding in Him we might bear fruit.

Drawing inspiration from the "fruits of the Spirit" enumerated in Galatians 5 (love, joy, peace, patience, kindness, goodness, faith, gentleness, and self-control), this series is devoted to cultivating fruit in the life of a believer.

In this series of meditations and sermons on the Fruit of the Spirit, Christians will be challenged to measure spiritual success the way Jesus did – not according to religious activity, but according to the fruitfulness of our lives as we walk in the Spirit.

FOREWORD:
"ALL YOU NEED IS LOVE"

Isn't love what all human beings are in search of? We want the love of others – our parents, our spouse, our children. And we learn that we can earn this love if we behave, if we do certain things, if we meet their needs. There are all kinds of conditions placed on human love. According to Pastor Steve Babbitt, we have it all wrong. We're searching for love in all the wrong places. We first have to know and experience Holy Love before we can see growth in our human love. Mark 12:28-31 gives us the most important commandment: We are to love God with all our heart, soul, mind, and strength and love your neighbor as yourself.

In *Love Never Fails*, Pastor Steve gives us the roadmap to love. He contrasts human love which always fails, to God's Holy Love that never fails. By providing real life experiences to which we can all relate, Steve explains how we must first know we are loved by God and then love Him back. Only then can we see the difference in our human love. God loves us unconditionally; unlike any human love we know. God loves you just the way you are. Steve demonstrates how, unlike human love, Holy Love is our path to freedom. He shows us how Holy Love is a love than doesn't need to be earned; God gives it to us freely.

In Part Three of Steve's book, we see how knowing God loves us and accepting His love and loving Him back with our heart, soul, mind and strength will then be reflected in our lives. Steve shares the importance of using our gifts, talents, and skills for the glory of God.

This book is a must read for all who search for true love, both God's Holy Love and loving, healthy human relationships. To see true love in our earthly relationships we must first know Holy Love. In his down to earth, honest way, Steve explains Holy Love. He shares stories to which we can all relate, as we journey towards strengthening our relationships – first and most importantly with God and then with others.

We have all made decisions that have changed our life. But have they been life changing? In a way we can all understand and relate to, Steve demonstrates how the decision to accept and return God's love will indeed change our life. He shows us how our spiritual life will be integrated with our personal life.

Like so many people, you may have been riding the fence for too long. Accepting God's love is *"a chance of a lifetime in a lifetime of chance – and it's time you joined the dance."*

Ed Poole, Ed.D.
Kathi Poole, Ed.D.
Authors, *Lessons from Empowering Leaders: Real Life Stories to Inspire Your Organization Toward Greater Success*

PROLOGUE:
WHERE HUMAN LOVE ENDS
& HOLY LOVE BEGINS

My favorite comedian, Brian Regan, has a sketch about losing his luggage at the airport. When he reports it to the airline, they give him a minuscule "essentials kit." Regan wryly remarks, "Why did I need all that other stuff? Right here in this little bag, I've got everything I need: food, shelter and love."

Food gives us strength. Shelter provides safety. Love gives us a reason. Love is now, and ever shall be, our most essential need. Take away food and shelter – even our very breath – and our need for love still remains. Take away love, however, and nothing remains.

The Bible promises us that *"love never fails." (1 Corinthians 13.8)*

Why is it, then, that love seems to fail at an alarming rate? Marriages fall apart. Children drift away. Friends become enemies. How dare the Bible claim that "love never fails"? What is malfunctioning with love? Why does it seem to **only** fail? Perhaps the love referenced in the Bible is different than the love we experience in daily life.

Human love fails.

Holy Love – the love Paul speaks of in 1 Corinthians 13 – *never fails*.

The following meditations aim to dismantle our broken concept of human love then rebuild it from the ground up so that we might enjoy perfect love – Holy Love that never fails.

In the Gospels, Jesus affirms that the two greatest commandments are to love God with all our heart, soul and strength, and to love our neighbor as ourselves. These were not new commands. Both leap from nearly every page of the Old Testament. In fact, Jesus says these two are the hinges on which hang the entire law (including the Ten Commandments) and all the prophets, including Isaiah, Jeremiah, Ezekiel, Daniel, and the rest.

You could rightly say that the upshot of the whole Bible is to **love God** and **love our neighbor.** Do these, Jesus says to the scribe in Luke 10, "and you will inherit eternal life." Of course, no one can love like this even part of the time, which is why we need the sin-for-life exchange of the cross. But, any reading of the New Testament reveals that, for those who follow Jesus, God's goal is for each of us to adopt this new way of Holy Love – even though it may be foreign to us.

Love In Three Dimensions

Based on the *Greatest Commandments* and the following *Parable of the Good Samaritan* in Luke 10.28-37, the meditations within focus on the three key dimensions where our concept of love needs the most extreme work.

First, we need to change the way we think about **being loved** – in particular, the way we think about being loved **by God.** I am going to argue that every fracture of human love springs from misunderstanding just how much God loves us.

If we have not properly **received** Holy Love, we cannot properly **give** Holy Love.

Second, before we attempt to love our neighbor (whether a spouse, parent, child, or enemy), the love we have received must first be **given back to God.** Jesus, the master of all love, prioritized "love the Lord your God" as the first and greatest commandment – for good reason!

We cannot love others **well** if we do not love God **first.**

Finally, once we've been firmly anchored in being loved by God and in returning His love, **love for our neighbor** can finally begin to take shape. This is where love is made manifest in our relationships. Happy marriages, solid friendships, and social justice find lasting power only in the enduring embrace of Holy Love.

If we do not love **our neighbor,** we do not love **God.**

Disclaimer

The meditations that follow are not a trivial handful of tips to improve your marriage, friendships, or relationships at school or work. We're going to dive much deeper than the surface-level symptoms of human love's brokenness. I intend to cut right to the heart and expose the root cause of every lamentable disfigurement of human love.

These meditations are not baby-aspirin. They are, if received fully, more on the order of radical gene therapy that can to alter our DNA altogether. My goal is to completely deconstruct our concept of human love and resurrect it as Holy Love.

In that sense, I suppose this manuscript could inspire you to take steps to improve your marriage, friendships, and other relationships! But if so, you'll have to extrapolate those real-world applications of Holy Love on your own. In this book I will invite you to step back – way back – to consider the bigger picture of love on a universal scale.

My prayer as you read this book is twofold. First, I sincerely hope you will be open to the idea that your love (and mine, for that matter) is hopelessly inadequate. Second, I hope you will discover firsthand the One Love that is more than adequate … the love that whispers volumes from the cross …

Holy Love that *never fails.*

And now, may the true author of Love that Never Fails speak to your heart through the foolishness of these feeble words. By the grace and power of the Holy Spirit, may we all learn to love *again, aright, and anew.*

Pastor Steve Babbitt
San Diego, California
November 2018

On one occasion an expert in the law stood up to test Jesus. 'Teacher,' he asked, 'what must I do to inherit eternal life?'

'What is written in the Law?' he replied. 'How do you read it?'

He answered, 'Love the Lord your God with all your heart and with all your soul and with all your strength and with all your mind'; and, 'Love your neighbor as yourself.'

'You have answered correctly,' Jesus replied. 'Do this and you will live.'

But he wanted to justify himself, so he asked Jesus, 'And who is my neighbor?'

In reply Jesus said:

'A man was going down from Jerusalem to Jericho, when he was attacked by robbers. They stripped him of his clothes, beat him and went away, leaving him half dead. A priest happened to be going down the same road, and when he saw the man, he passed by on the other side. So too, a Levite, when he came to the place and saw him, passed by on the other side. But a Samaritan, as he traveled, came where the man was; and when he saw him, he took pity on him. He went to him and bandaged his wounds, pouring on oil and wine. Then he put the man on his own donkey, brought him to an inn and took care of him. The next day he took out two denarii and gave them to the innkeeper. "Look after him," he said, "and when I return, I will reimburse you for any extra expense you may have."'

'Which of these three do you think was a neighbor to the man who fell into the hands of robbers?'

The expert in the law replied, 'The one who had mercy on him.'

Jesus told him, 'Go and do likewise.'

(LUKE 10.25-37)

CHAPTER ONE:
THE RELUCTANT SAMARITAN

It was a sweltering Sunday morning in September 2013. I was a foreigner, a vulnerable tourist on a bodacious adventure through the Holy Land, completely alone for miles and miles on the highway, cooling off in an air-conditioned Honda I had just rented in Jerusalem. The radio's seek function yielded a single, fuzzy, pop station – in Arabic. I could almost make out the tune through the static. It sounded familiar, maybe a Tom Petty tune?

I was incredibly blessed to have a few days alone to simply spend time with God as I toured the Biblical sites I had read about and studied for so many years. I had been looking forward to this part of my trip for months.

Jericho loomed on the plain below as three defeated-looking hitchhikers came into view. I had no time for hitchhikers. Those strangers were not going to distract me from my self-righteous pilgrimage. Not today. So, I passed them by.

As I sped down the next steep curve toward the barren flatlands below, quite comfortable in my complacency, my Heavenly Friend went to work on me.

"It's Sunday," He said.

"We've got a lot to do," I replied. I put the pedal down to make some time.

"You're literally on Jericho Road," He answered. "You're an outsider – you know, kind of like a *Samaritan.* Come on, Steve, don't you see it?"

I attempted to justify myself. "I'm all alone. I'm in a country where people walk around with machine guns. I'm heading right into the occupied territories. I'm not going to risk getting killed."

"You're a **pastor**," He said, resting His case and looking away.

He always does this.

We gazed out the windshield silently together, scanning the hot brown expanse far below for a glimpse of that beautiful green oasis – Jericho, the City of Palms.

I reached the sleepy intersection at the bottom of the long grade, just a few hundred feet shy of the Jordan River. I paused there for quite a while, debating with myself a little longer. Finally, I made a U-turn and trudged back up the road a few miles to where I had passed the hitchhikers earlier.

The two men and a woman, scraggly twenty-somethings with dusty backpacks and mottled hair, were still thumbing for a ride. An uneasy cloud of questions formed in my head.

"What had they done to the last driver that resulted in being dumped here of all places? Who left them out in the middle of this blistering desert, in this terrible spot, on this dangerous mountain road?" I rolled down the window. "Get in."

My Heavenly Friend turned to look me in the eye. He smiled, knowing He had won the argument.

They collapsed into the seats. Exhausted from the heat, guzzling water from the bottles I shared with them.

"Z-zanks," stammered one of the young men.

For the first time in my travels, I encountered a group of people in another country where none them spoke even a little bit of English. We strained to communicate as I kept one eye on the road and the other on the two "thugs" in the backseat, who seemed bigger now.

The tired-looking woman in front saw I was nervous and tried to dismantle my concerns, explaining in "Hebrenglish" and made-up sign language that they were hitchhikers on vacation just touring the country-side. She claimed they were all Israeli.

This made it seem even more odd to me that they didn't speak English. Yet, I feebly convinced myself of my safety. "It's possible that an Israeli family could raise a child in complete isolation from the outside world," I thought.

In a short time we arrived at the Jordan again, where I dropped the girl and one of the young men off at Jericho. The last hitchhiker stayed with me as far as the Dead Sea Scrolls exhibit at Qumran, a few miles south. We shook hands and he disappeared into the visitor center.

Finally, I could get back to loving God. But I wondered: could I have authentically loved God on that day's journey without loving those ragtag "neighbors" as well?[1]

Strangers at Home

It took a foreigner to lend those hitchhikers a hand. Where were their countrymen? Where were their neighbors? It struck me that, even in their homeland, they were strangers.

How sad.

But isn't that true for each of us as well? In the city, we might sleep with just a thin wall separating us from a family of perfect strangers. In the country, we could visit the same convenience store for twenty years before we introduce ourselves to the tired face behind the counter. How many of us spend our time on earth as complete strangers, even at home?

Our neighbors are not *really* our neighbors. We belt out *All You Need is Love* with sincere conviction when we're alone in the car, yet we refuse to prove that conviction when we're alone and notice someone needing help. We might agree that sharing what we've got to help another person is a good idea – but only in principle.

In practice, we all assign our own needs the highest priority. With sincere apologies to Mr. Lennon and Mr. Lenin: despite your noteworthy efforts, neighborly love may still be *philosophically* alive today, but it is, on many fronts, *practically dead.*

If the Scriptures promise that *love never fails,* why is it that when we look at the world around us, love *always* seems to fail?

---

1 Looking back on this story years later, I suspect they may have been recent graduates serving their mandatory time in the Israeli Defense Forces (IDF), perhaps looking for suspicious vehicles, like mine, to investigate. I certainly didn't fit the profile of the average American bus-bound tourist that day, which may explain the numerous security checks I underwent over the course of the next week as I traveled throughout the rest of Israel and the West Bank in that trusty little Honda.

Why do people still die alone in crowded neighborhoods? Why are there more great weddings, but fewer good marriages? Why are there more human beings today, but less humanity?

It seems to me that our "love problem" actually lies with the *kind* of love we have. We don't need more of the same kind of love; we need love of a different variety altogether. We need ***Holy Love.***

Constant Contraction

Human love is little more than a clever counterfeit of Holy Love. It is a copy of the original – sometimes convincing, but ultimately a forgery of the great love that is God. Where Holy Love is always expanding its reach, human love is always contracting and shrinking, seeking out border walls to build. Because human love is always defined by borders, human love fails miserably and offers no hope of victory over the darkness. Holy Love never fails.

Human love has eversmall limits. There is always a boundary human love will refuse to cross; a county line where its jurisdiction ends. Human love refuses to tread certain turf. Human love is different from Holy Love because it is constrained by the fence of human fear.

The Tri-fold Limits of Human Love

First, human love limits our understanding of ***God's love for us*** because it is constrained by the self-prescribed boundaries of insecurity. We cannot receive the Holy Love of God if we cannot get past the roadblocks of our own, often well-deserved, guilt and shame. Unholy human love simply cannot comprehend the full breadth, height, and depth of God's forgiving and restoring love. Human love's tape measure simply can't reach that far.

Second, human love limits ***our love for God*** because it is crushed behind the punishing curtain of religion. Few counterfeits are as clever as religion. Foxhole confessions are short-lived. Worship and praise music makes more disciples of ***hype*** than of the ***Holy Ghost.*** Our finest offerings easily masquerade as love for God when they may be nothing of the sort. If anything, religion is more often worship of the self – an attempt to scratch a spiritual itch or complete a religio-social checklist – rather than a genuine display of love for God. Human love always fails to grasp how we might truly love God – heart, soul, and strength.

Third, human love limits our understanding of *love for our neighbor* because it is hamstrung by the crippling borders of prejudice. We simply *don't care* about our neighbors. Sometimes we are even awash in loathing for them. Human love keeps tedious records of every wrong and zooms in on every unpleasant cultural difference, no matter how innocent, failing to grasp how we ought to love our neighbor the way we love ourselves.

Human love fails 100% of the time. It might take a while to discover the wreckage, but without exception, human love is just a sinking ship.

I would like to propose a different kind of love – I call it Holy Love.

Tear Down That Wall

In contrast to worldly human love is the Holy Love of God. This is the divine original, which human love so clumsily models itself after.

Holy Love fears no region of the human experience. It is the law that is written on all of our hearts. It is the love that we all know we ought to share, but can never quite express in full. Holy Love is the ideal that human love so feebly attempts to copy. It is the love we are urged to exercise in the Lord's great commands to love God heart, soul, and strength, and love our neighbor as ourselves.

Holy Love – the *uncut original* – is excellently played out for us in the story of the Good Samaritan, which is about expanding human love's borders until they evaporate entirely, raising the curtain to reveal Holy Love. When the beaten man is discovered by his own Hebrew countrymen – the Priest and the Levite – they are compelled to ignore him for religious reasons. The Priest and Levite would become "ceremonially unclean" if either was to touch a corpse. If the man died while they cared for his wounds, their religion would quarantine them for a few days.

Loving their neighbor was, quite simply, an inconvenience. So, they passed by on the other side of the road in a perfect example of human love's imperfection.

In contrast stands the Good Samaritan. Let's look at the boundaries the Samaritan – Holy Love's archetype – so willingly crossed.

The Samaritan had to *give of himself.* And notice how much he gave! First, he poured soothing oil and healing wine on the man's wounds. Then he gave from his own modest supply to wrap the man's wounds with bandages.

He could have stopped there, but he gave more. He gave up his donkey to portage the man to Jericho and the Inn. He could have stopped there, but he gave more. He stayed at the stranger's bedside to care for him. He could have stopped there, but still he gave more. He prepaid the innkeeper for a few extra nights. He didn't stop there,rather, he gave more, promising to return in a few days' time and cover any extra charges.

The Samaritan **gave** sacrificially – not a little, but with unconscionable abundance; not once, but continuously. Time, money, schedule, safety, ego … all were placed, without hesitation, on the altar of sacrifice, and all in the name of Holy Love.

In order for the Samaritan to tear down the border walls of human love by giving of himself, he had to **get over himself.**

The beaten victim was Jewish, and nationalistic Hebrews of that era had no dealings with the people of Samaria. Palestine is wretchedly divided by some in the same ways to this day.

It was a great cultural risk for the Samaritan to break social ranks and be seen caring for a Samaritan-despising Hebrew. But the Samaritan, again, is a perfect model of Holy Love. Holy Love is not saddled with the burdens of culture and peer pressure. Holy Love is perfectly willing to transcend societal norms in order to manifest God's new society – the kingdom of Heaven – on Earth.

Finally, the Samaritan had to **get dirty** in the name of Holy Love – even putting his life on the line. He was not worried about contamination or the danger that the wounded man might be part of a trap. He simply did the right thing by getting close to the victim he found on the side of the road regardless of any risk.

Faith or Fear?

We only live in one of two ways: in faith or in fear.

Fear usually presents itself as a convincing counterfeit of faith. In truth, however, it serves a puny god and comes up with every excuse to refrain from showing Holy Love to a neighbor. "That neighborhood is too rough. Their school is too poor. Their views are different from mine."

Such contrived excuses are not evidence of faith, but proof of fear pretending to be practical. Fear is always looking for a wall to build. Fear relies on an arsenal of well-reasoned excuses to ignore God's command to love our enemies. Fear – especially fear disguised behind the mask of Christian words – thinks God is weak and cannot handle Himself in the face of real-world challenges.

Genuine faith, on the other hand, trusts that God can handle all obstacles and will guide and protect us wherever He calls us to serve in love. Faith is not worried about getting dirty or getting hurt because it knows God got very dirty himself when He came to earth to save us, and that there is no hurt that compares to the hurt Jesus willingly embraced at the cross.

Jericho Road is Dangerous

The road to Jericho represents our journey to Holy Love. The road to Holy Love is not an easy one. It is fraught with frustration, pitfalls, and perils. Bandits lurk around most corners. The personal cost of traveling to Holy Love can be steep on that snaking mountain road.

In spite of the dangers, Holy Love refuses to give primacy to safety as the Priest and Levite did. Holy Love is willing to risk the possibility of being injured on the journey, exemplified in the man on the cross. The Lord Jesus Christ knew it would be dangerous to confront the shallowness of human love by coming to earth and manifesting Holy Love among us.

The incarnation was not easy for Jesus. He faced real danger, discomfort, and denigration at every turn. Did Holy Love shrug off the mission? Did it shy away from the opportunity? No! God the Father stepped out in Holy Love, risked everything to send His Son so that we might live, and sealed us with the power of the Holy Spirit so that we might love Him – and one another – with Holy Love. To love with holiness means to risk all.[2]

---

2 I'm aware that this could be misunderstood as a mandate for victims of abuse to remain in abusive relationships. Holy Love utterly abhors systemic abuse and refuses to tolerate it. I certainly don't think the Lord is calling victims of abuse to continue to allow their victimizers to beat them down. In fact, Holy Love mandates that all abusers called into account for their wicked deeds, and that they bear the societal consequences of their actions. Victims of abuse should do everything within their power to escape the abuse, and we in the church should do everything in our power to assist them. Human love cherishes perpetual victimhood, Holy Love works to put an end to violence.

Gateway to the Promised Land

Jericho, the destination in our story of the Good Samaritan, is a key setting in the Scriptures. Most importantly, the City of Palms figured as the gateway to the promised land after the Exodus. Joshua and the children of Israel first entered the land of milk and honey through Jericho. Spiritually, Jericho represents the sacred ground we all must pass as we enter God's promised land.

In the Good Samaritan tale, the road to Jericho is transformed into the road of mercy, the place where Hebrew and Samaritan divest themselves of enmity and adopt a spirit of neighborliness.

This is the road that we are called to travel – the road to Jericho; the road of Holy Love.

There is another "Good Samaritan" story found deep in the archives of the Old Testament, and it contains striking similarities. In 2 Chronicles Chapter 28, the Samarian prophet Oded demanded that his people release 200,000 Judean prisoners of war – men, women and children – who had been badly beaten.

In that story, we find some of the same elements as in Jesus's story of the Good Samaritan. The Samaritans, under conviction by Oded, provide oil for wounds and donkeys to carry the weak prisoners home. Their destination, too, was Jericho, the City of Palms.

In the story of Oded, however, the emphasis extends beyond identifying Hebrew and Samaritan as neighbors to the more grand themes of freedom and ransom. In Oded's case, captives are not only recognized as neighbors – they were *set free.* Freedom is found as we travel the road of mercy, loving our neighbor. Coincidence? I think not. When telling of the Good Samaritan, Jesus was almost surely alluding to the story of Oded to make His case to the teacher of the law attempting to trap Him.

This should give us pause. Perhaps there is more than mere kindness at stake when we put ourselves in the shoes of the Good Samaritan. When we stretch into the vastness of Holy Love and strive to see our enemies as neighbors *we are also setting them – and ourselves – free.* Could it be that, as in the case of Oded, when we care deeply for our enemies – though they may hate us with all their heart, soul and strength – we are really destroying the chains of enmity?

Thus the road to Jericho – the narrow path of Holy Love – is not merely the road to neighborly love; it is ultimately the road to freedom. Freedom from the confines of man-made labels. Freedom from the internal struggle of self-loathing. And most of all, freedom from the borders wrought by unholy fear.

If we attempt to make it to Jericho on the fumes of human love, that great oasis will always remain out of reach. If we learn to travel the way of Holy Love, we will always get home.

"For God so loved
the world ..."

(JOHN 3.16A)

PART ONE:
BEING LOVED

What a wonderful promise! "God so loved the world." Could there be better news than that?

Let's be honest though. What is there to "so love" about the world? And for that matter, what is there to "so love" about *any* of us? Sure, we have good days. Everyone loves hearing diamond-in-the-slag stories of human love weathering bitter life-storms. But, it seems that for every sweet story of human love, a dozen bitter tales of human frailty follow. School shootings, political intrigue, wars – and rumors of them. Even the seemingly "good" people who show human love for a season eventually devolve into abuse and hatred.

Human love is, sadly, unsustainable. It comes and goes. A husband may be kind in the morning and a monster at night. A celebrity may take a stand against injustice on Friday and be exposed as a sexual predator on Monday. A wife may hurriedly drop off cookies for the school bake sale on her way to a clandestine meeting with a man who's not her husband.

Human love *always* fails.

The kind of love that we can generate on our own is simply unreliable, unpredictable, and unsustainable. The weeping prophet Jeremiah deftly prosecuted our tawdry hearts when he said, *"The heart is deceitful above all things, and beyond cure. Who can understand it?" (Jeremiah 17.9)*

Pretending to be Found

In Brennan Manning's marvel of a book, *Abba's Child*, he calls us all *frauds* pretending to be good boys and girls on the outside, when we are desperately wicked on the inside. We say we are found, even when we are completely lost.

Those of us who have made it our aim to go against societal norms and "surrender all" to Jesus (in the name of love, mind you) still find ourselves floundering to respond to rejection with love more than a fraction of the time.

When all pretending is stripped away – when you tally up your own personal record of rights and wrongs – I have a hunch that you, like me, will come to the same conclusion: we as a species are, on the whole, miserable and ultimately... honestly... tragically... ***unloveworthy.***

Not unlov*able*; unlove*worthy*. There is a cosmic difference.

If we can muster the courage to drop the charade and be honest with ourselves, we will ultimately realize that there is ***not so much*** for God to "***so love.***"

And yet, those ageless words still pierce my darkness and yours. *"God so loved the world."*

God's Word never lies – and there it is, written in permanent ink. *"God so loved ..."*

You.

And me.

And the husband who is a monster at night.

And the celebrity who is a predator.

And the wife who cheats on her husband.

And every other scoundrel and fraud on the face of the earth.

Which means that:

God so loved the world.

God so loved all of us.

God so loved ***you***.

Before we get to parts two and three of this book on loving God and neighbor, I invite you to step back and start at the very beginning. Before

---

we give love we need to receive it. We need to drink living water from the source, where everlasting Holy Love triumphs over weak-kneed human love.

"But God demonstrates
his own love for us in this:
While we were still sinners,
Christ died for us."
(ROMANS 5.8)

CHAPTER TWO:
BELOVED WITHOUT A CAUSE

I am a pastor. Each week I am granted the task of carefully studying the sacred and stirring Word of God as revealed in the Scriptures – to soak my feeble and dry mind in the living water of the Holy Spirit before delivering a word or two that will hopefully, by God's grace and power, encourage His people.

Not long ago I was preparing to talk about our mission as the people of God, revealed in Luke 10.25-28, that we are commissioned to love God with all our heart and soul, mind, and strength; and to love our neighbor as ourselves.

As I was preparing my sermon, my friend Gidgitte warned me, "Steve, you *cannot begin to love God or your neighbor until you know that you are loved by God first.*"

She was speaking through the Holy Spirit.

After all, how can we bake bread if we are out of flour? How can you invest in a business if you are bankrupt yourself? How can you make a marriage work if you are musclebound with insecurity? How can we love anyone – God or neighbor – if we do not know for certain that we ourselves are beloved?

A marriage is doomed to fail when one or both partners pin their sense of identity and value on the other's capacity to love. Human love is feeble and imperfect, but there is One who loves us truly and infallibly.

A wife needs to know she is loved by God more deeply than her husband can ever love her if she is to rest soundly in his shallower affections – even if well-meaning.

A husband needs to grasp that his worth comes from being loved by the Almighty, not from the wavering adoration of his wife – even if sincere. A marriage built on human love alone is only one minor tremor away from falling apart.

It would be a mistake to think that humans have more than a meager capacity to love God and neighbor. Because human love is frail and unsustainable, we cannot even talk about loving God and neighbor before first learning, and accepting, that we are beloved by God.

Human love cannot truly love God. Human love cannot fully love neighbor. Human love cannot inexhaustibly love a husband, wife, child, or enemy.

Only Divine love – **only Holy Love** – can love without fail.

Rebel Without a Because

The critical thing to notice about John 3.16 is that there is no "because."

The significance of that should knock us to the ground. When it comes to God "so loving" you and me **there is no obvious "because"**. There is no reason. No list of pros and cons.

We are merely and simply beloved.

In contrast, human love always needs a "because." There is always a string attached. There is always a reason, always a trick up the sleeve, always a stipulation or manipulation in play.

"I love you *because* you are so kind to me."

"I love you *because* you are beautiful."

"I love you *because* I think I can change you."

On the other hand, Holy Love is foreign and unconstrained by conditionality. God the Father is the ultimate rebel who loves without a "because". When there is every reason **not** to "so love the world," God the Father loves us anyway!

We are, simply, beloved.

So what does that mean to the ragtag and wounded people of God who band together in the name of this Love? I think the questions should be obvious. Do we *trust* that we are "so loved" by God? And do we **know** that He loves us **without a "because"**? Have we considered that every "because" we offer Him is just clutter, static, and trouble on the line?

Our list of reasons why God should love us, whether spoken or covert, are worthless prattle. Our sacrifices do not mean anything to Him.

It is *you* He wants, not your offerings. **You** mean everything to Him.

Have you been doing good deeds to gain God's approval? You're wasting your time. They are rubble. Have you been singing praises in church and reciting Scripture to get His attention? It's all babble. We've been wasting our time trying to earn something that is already ours in abundance. We already have His attention. We already have His adoration. **We already have His love.**

Doing our religious duty has no bearing on His love for us. He loves the buttoned-up you on Sunday morning, sober and ready to hear from Him, just the same as He loves the intoxicated you on Saturday night, bound to the couch after a night of regrettable choices.

His love keeps no record of wrongs. It always perseveres — *just because.*

Gong Show Religion

The apostle Paul says that religion – if God's love is not the center of it – is like a "resounding gong or a clanging cymbal." (1 Corinthians 13.1b) Which, for me, always brings to mind *The Gong Show.*

As a kid growing up in the 1970s, I loved watching *The Gong Show* with Chuck Barris. If you're not familiar, it was a low-budget version of *Star Search,* which, if you're not familiar, was a low-budget version of *American Idol,* which was a low-budget version of *America's Got Talent,* which was a low-budget version of *The Voice...* History always repeats itself – just with a bigger budget.

On *The Gong Show,* amateur performers would sing, dance, and tell jokes before a panel of three judges sitting in front of an enormous gong. If any of the judges didn't like the act, they would bang the gong and a giant hook would come out and drag performers off stage. It was funny (unless, of course, you were the one who got "gonged")!

Paul says that religion without God's love is basically just another *Gong Show*. Without Holy Love, we are little more than nervous contestants desperately trying to avoid religion's hook. Without the security of God's unfailing love, we live in fear of being dragged offstage because we suspect that even our best performances may not be impressive enough.

Religion can be quite merciless, excluding those who don't sing and dance according to its capricious standards.

But God's love – Holy Love – has no gong. The Love of God is not based on the quality of our performance. Jesus didn't die on a sliding scale. Your actions – good or bad – cannot alter the historical event of the crucifixion where we discover irrefutable evidence of God's love for all humanity. At the cross, God the Father demonstrated once and for all that He simply "so loved" the world.

No because. No score sheet. No record of rights violations, no record of wrongs.

And no manipulation. ***He just loves you as you are.***

Bandages Off

Brennan Manning, again in *Abba's Child*, calls our religious costumes "bandages." As little more than glittering plastic sequins of surface good deeds and the cheap crackling rhinestones of human righteousness, our costumes are not at all impressive to God. Indeed, the Bible calls even our most righteous deeds "filthy rags." (Isaiah 64.6)

In order to really understand the "so love" of God, we need to peel off those bandages, get out of our costumes, and discard our filthy rags. We need to stop trying to impress one another and God, stop being imposters and start simply being loved – *"so loved"* – by God.

Jesus, at the cross, is our ultimate model of vulnerability without pretense.

At the cross – in that shameful, shameless, naked, and vulnerable place – all that remains is you; the real you, the one underneath the smothering coverings of duty, accomplishments, obedience, and every other impotent attempt to earn love.

At the cross – where God's love is demonstrated *once and for all of us* – every "because" we might claim is found to be baseless and fraudulent. There is no "because" that can explain the absurd fortune of the Son of God torn to pieces in our stead. No one deserves that; no one is that good. Such a soaring ransom is unthinkable.

You are merely and simply beloved.

While we've been toiling away at the endless spinning wheel of achievement – trying to earn God's favor and the approval of others – we have missed the fact that our achievements only get in the way.

The Most Foolish of Fool's Gold

We are beloved only because God loves us, and never because of anything we have done. We are like gold miners, scratching away in deep, dark pits, trying to muscle God's love out of unforgiving rock when all the while, gold bars are lying around on the surface.

Even children understand this, and they are rich until they fall for the lie that there is more gold to be found by clawing underground in the mines of duty and religion. May we become like little children again!

According to Jeremiah, there are three kinds of fool's gold to be found in mines of human effort: *wealth, wisdom* and *works.*

> *"'Let not the wise boast of their wisdom*
> *or the strong boast of their strength*
> *or the rich boast of their riches,*
> *but let the one who boasts boast about this:*
> *that they have the understanding to know me,*
> *that I am the Lord, who exercises kindness,*
> *justice and righteousness on earth,*
> *for in these I delight,'*
> *declares the Lord."*
> *(Jeremiah 9.23–24)*

Wealth Can't Coerce God into Loving Us

> *"Let not the rich boast of their riches..."*
> *(Jeremiah 9.23)*

The Joneses next door might be impressed with your car and your clothes, but God yawns at such trivia. We live in a world where human love is bought with money. But one day the scriptures promise that everything we possess will either melt or burn – no other option.

Then what will we have?

God's word, however, will stand forever – the word that promises "God so loved" us. We may be living in a material world, but God is looking for immaterial girls and boys who understand that His love is not based on anything they possess. You simply cannot buy God's love.

God doesn't accept bribes, not even small ones.

Wisdom Can't Convince God to Love Us

"Let not the wise boast of their wisdom…"
(Jeremiah 9.23)

Good grades, advanced degrees, and letters after our names are much-desired in this world, but they mean precious little in the sight of God. While the world heaps praises on the smart and the gifted, God bestows the ultimate gift on those who simply receive His love.

No persuasive essay can bend God. No diploma can ever be gained that will merit His favor. No written test can be passed that will permit us to cruise with Him down life's highway. Human wisdom and knowledge are utterly fallible, but God's love for us never fails.

Works Can't Compel God to Love Us

"Let not the strong boast of their strength…"
(Jeremiah 9.23)

We know that we are saved by grace through faith, and not by deeds that anyone should boast. But we sure like to boast anyway!

I know of some churches that issue press releases whenever they feed the homeless or do a good deed. They shout their own accolades from the street corners and from their Instagram accounts. While it is definitely good to be so good, according to Jesus, they already have their reward. (Matthew 6.2)

The only reward worth pursuing is the love of God. There is nothing else that compares to the priceless award of being loved by Him. All of our deeds mean nothing without the "because-less" love of God.

Welcome Back to the Garden

Perhaps I have been too critical of wealth and wisdom and works. Each one actually has its proper place *in the service* of God. But they must never be mistaken for the *price of admission* to God's love.

At the foot of the cross:

- All resumes are shredded.
- All possessions are repossessed.
- All clearances are revoked.
- All accomplishments are obliterated.
- All achievements are ignored.
- All failures are forgotten.

After all is said and done, we are only able to stand because we are profoundly, mysteriously, and *completely loved.*

"Love never fails."
(1 CORINTHIANS 13.8)

CHAPTER THREE:

LOVE LIKE DAY AND NIGHT

First Corinthians 13, "The Love Chapter," is used in weddings as a way to describe human love, but if we look closer, the love described here is not like human love at all. A love that "keeps no record of wrongs" doesn't sound like most relationships I know. A love that's patient and always trusts isn't the kind of love we experience with other people. Suppose The Love Chapter is not a picture of human love, but a description of **God's Holy Love.**

It describes love of a different breed. The quality of God's love for us is nothing like the quality of love that we humans have for one another. Human love is derivative – a hazy copy of the original. Human love is, as Paul says, a shabby and "tainted reflection" of the Holy Love we were created to inhabit.

And yet the love of God is what we strive to emulate as we consider what it means to love God and our neighbor. This ideal version of love is modeled for us here in 1 Corinthians 13. Not only does this passage in the sacred text show us how we ought to love others, but it also describes the way **God loves us.** What if we were to re-read 1 Corinthians 13 with fresh eyes, looking not merely for inspiration on how we ought to love others, but also with a mind to discovering the way that God loves us?

The following paraphrase is my amateur attempt to emphasize that aspect of the inspired Word. My prayer is that Holy Love's example may update the rhythm of your own heart as you read.

Nothing Without Love (Verses 1-3)

"If I speak in the tongues of men or of angels, but do not have love, I am only a resounding gong or a clanging cymbal."

If I utter nonsense babblings on one hand and deliver clever, pie-in-the-sky rhetoric on the other, but have not listened to the truth that I am first and foremost a beloved child of God, every syllable sputters. If I don't first understand that my maker loves me regardless of any jig my tongue can dance, I am a smash-mouthed nothing; just a banging gong or a choppy cymbal; a piano way out of tune; a guitar with broken strings; a concert violinist fidgeting with a shredded bow.

"If I have the gift of prophecy and can fathom all mysteries and all knowledge, and if I have a faith that can move mountains, but do not have love, I am nothing."

If I can rightly divide the Word of God with the best of them, teach so skillfully that even a child can understand the Four Spiritual Laws, the Romans Road, and even the mighty book of Revelation … If I can do all that, but somehow manage to miss the point of all of those messages – that I am loved by God – I have utterly lost the plot.

If I am a real brainiac holding a Bible in one hand and a dung-pile of degrees in the other…

If I am the one people always seem to come to for answers…

If I flatter myself into thinking I have more than half a clue about the wisdom of God...

If I do all that yet I somehow fail to grasp the most important truth – that God loves me –

If I don't get that "God so loved the world" means "God so loved me"... I am beyond ignorant.

If I have a faith that can move mountains …

If I have seen God's power manifested in ways that would make your innards loop-the-loop…

If I trust God so much that I have the courage to step out into parts unknown, but don't have the greater courage to simply trust that He loves me...

Whatever I accomplish is meaningless.

Those mountains may as well have never moved in the first place. God's love has much better things to do than relocate rock piles.

⎯⎯⎯⎯⎯⎯⎯⎯⎯•《◉》•⎯⎯⎯⎯⎯⎯⎯⎯⎯

"If I give all I possess to the poor and give over my body to hardship that I may boast, but do not have love, I gain nothing."

⎯⎯⎯⎯⎯⎯⎯⎯⎯•《◉》•⎯⎯⎯⎯⎯⎯⎯⎯⎯

If I give all I possess to the poor …

If my financial offerings would make Mother Teresa seem like a selfish, fat-cat Wall Street tycoon …

If I am so obedient to God's decrees for social justice that I give til it hurts and then a little more…

If I stand up against human trafficking, care for every widow and orphan I meet, and march for the rights of unborn human children, but somehow lose sight of the fact that God "so loved me"...

I may have done some good, but I have lost my hold on the one thing that matters most.

If I give over my body to the flames so that I may boast …

If I am unafraid to stand up and testify to God's love in the hostile courtroom of today's culture …

If I am so unashamed of the Gospel of Christ that people throw rocks at me, can't stand to be around me, shut me out, unfriend me, cut me out of the will, persecute me …

If I am one of those people who don't care what you think about me, just as long as I get a chance to share the message…

If I do all this for Jesus, but never comprehend how His own suffering was borne out of His deep affection for me …

I gain less than zero.

A Different Breed of Love (Verses 4-7)

"Love is patient, love is kind. It does not envy, it does not boast, it is not proud."

God's love for me is patient. He isn't pushy. No one can love in a hurry. His love doesn't force me to do anything, to be anywhere, to pick up the pace. When I'm stuck in life's traffic, He is happy to be stuck there too.

God's limitless love for me is kind. He's never going to dress me down for wearing the wrong thing or embarrass me by dragging out my past. He isn't out to make me look bad. I am a co-heir to His throne, and He treats me like it. He knows my faults, and He chooses to stay with me just the same.

God is secure in Himself. He is slow to anger when I stray. He waits patiently while I worship at the mall of materialism, build a shrine to myself, and seek my own praise on social media. He is jealous for me, but not like an insecure bully.[3]

God's love for me does not boast. He isn't in it for the attention – I'll never be some cheap prize to Him. He would love me the same if there was

---

3 This section – "love does not envy" – is the part of this exposition that I am least comfortable with. If, as I'm arguing, Holy Love is the same as God's love, and Holy Love does not envy, how do we reconcile that with the Scriptures where God is described as a "jealous" God? It may help to differentiate between envy and jealousy. Envy is personal ("I desire to be who they are"), whereas jealousy is possessional ("I desire to have what they have"). Jealousy wants to have something it doesn't have. Envy wants to be someone it is not. In that sense, God can be "jealous" of the affections we have for other "gods" while not "envying," or desiring to be, those false gods. In any case, the idea of God being "jealous" is probably best understood, at least in part, as an anthropomorphism intended to encourage faithfulness and exclusive affection for the one true God.

---

no one else in the world to notice.

The love God has for me is not too proud to get dirty. To be with me, He would walk 500 miles and then walk 500 more. He would charge across the raging sea. He would give up all His heavenly glory and dwell with me. He was willing to suffer shame and humiliation on Calvary – all for the sake of His love for me.

———···———

"It does not dishonor others, it is not self-seeking, it is not easily angered, it keeps no record of wrongs."

———···———

God's love for me does not put others down. He loves everyone I live with, everyone I work with, and everyone I despise just as much as He loves me. Who am I to judge my neighbor? My family, my enemies, and my friends are all loved by God just the same way I am – without limit.

God's love is not self-seeking. He is never so busy with "important" things that He doesn't make time for me. If He was testifying before Congress and I called, He would shush the chairperson and pick up the phone. I am never an interruption. I am important to Him.

God's love for me is not easily angered – and am I ever glad for that! I didn't say "never angered," just "not easily" angered. And only ever **righteously** angered, which is something I am very thankful for.

God's love for me keeps no record of wrongs – even though I insist on keeping a stack of disappointing scorecards in my top drawer. Why do I replay my failures when He has erased them all, blotting out every last one?

———···———

"Love does not delight in evil but rejoices with the truth."

———···———

God's love does not tolerate injustice, and it demands that the truth be told. Just because He loves me doesn't mean I don't disappoint Him when I make bad choices. It tears Him apart when I do what is wrong, when I harm myself, or Him, or others in word or deed. But by the same token, He rockets through the roof with joy when I say and do the right things. He gives a standing ovation when I work to expose injustice.

"It always protects, always trusts, always hopes, always perseveres."

God's love always protects me. Life's storms are too dangerous to face alone. I need shelter, and that's exactly what God's love is. I must swallow my pride and take refuge in His everlasting arms.

God's love always trusts me enough to give me another chance – even if I've dropped the ball a thousand times.

God's love always hopes for the best – even if my life has been a tragedy of errors. His love hopes in me, especially when I have given up on myself.

God's love for me always perseveres, even when the road gets long. More tenacious than a bulldog, God's love never gives up. Ever!

Reflections and Remains (Verses 8-13)

"Love never fails. But where there are prophecies, they will cease; where there are tongues, they will be stilled; where there is knowledge, it will pass away."

God's love for me never fails. He never runs out of fuel. He never runs out of faith. He never gets tired. He never lets up. He never lets go.

But where there are prophecies and pamphlets, TV preachers and big tent revivals, they will cease. Who needs them anyway? The love of God flowing through me is more persuasive than ten thousand big tent revivals.

Where there are tongues and TED talks and preachers that ooze spirituality, they will be canceled. All of mankind's videos will eventually be paused, stopped, and deleted – but the love of God loops brighter and brighter forever.

Where there is knowledge and people are high on intellectualism, where people mistake the task of Bible memorization for the journey of discipleship – such things will pass away. God doesn't care about my IQ. The love of God sails right on by the mothballed ships of mankind's flim-flam knowledge. Learning disabilities or brain injuries or dementia could never separate us from the love of God.

***

"For we know in part and we prophesy in part ..."

***

For I understand just a little, and I speak just a little more. But I can't help struggling to comprehend a love so bold. It is just too breathlessly vast for me to imagine. I struggle once again to proclaim this kind of love to others and somehow do it justice. All of my words fall short; so for now, at least, I must be content just to scratch away at the surface.

***

"... but when completeness comes, what is in part disappears."

***

When Holy Love is finally revealed, my concept of human love will evaporate forever. One day, when Heaven comes to earth, I will stop splashing in the shallows and I shall touch the ocean floor.

***

"When I was a child, I talked like a child, I thought like a child, I reasoned like a child. When I became a man, I put the ways of childhood behind me."

***

When I was a kid, everything was a game. When I grew up, I stopped playing games. When I finally came of age, I couldn't wait to take off the training wheels. I opened my heart and my soul, my mind and my strength, to bigger and better things. Thank God, I finally grew up!

———◦((◦))◦———

"For now we see only a reflection as in a mirror; then we shall see face to face. Now I know in part; then I shall know fully, even as I am fully known."

———◦((◦))◦———

And so it is with the love of God. For today we see only a reflection of His love in the dingy mirror universe of human love; but then we shall stand face to face with the real article. Now I have only half the puzzle. Everything we know of God's love for us in this life is just a sample-spoonful. But then… oh then! Then we will feast on His love until we pop. Now we sip through the stir-straw of human love, then we will drink from the fire hose of Holy Love. When God's love is revealed, we shall know Him in full, even as He wraps us in His embrace now.

———◦((◦))◦———

"And now these three remain: faith, hope and love. But the greatest of these is love."

———◦((◦))◦———

When all else passes away and all the crust of religion is gone – three things will remain undefeated: faith, hope and love.

But the greatest of these three – that epic wave I've just got to catch – is God's love for me.

"Love does not
rejoice at injustice, but
rejoices with the truth."
(1 CORINTHIANS 13.6)

CHAPTER FOUR:
How Far, Love?

Uneasy Extravagance

At this point you may be thinking, "Enough. I get it. I understand – I am beloved."

But the truth is, we probably never will understand on this side of glory. The river of God's love for us is far deeper than any of us imagined.

This kind of love is beautiful, rare, and precious. It is exactly the kind of love that the world – and you and I – need. A love both *supreme* and *extreme.*

But we might feel uneasy about the extravagance of such a love.

"What about the evil in the world? If Holy Love exists, can it tolerate so much injustice? Surely the Scriptures teach us that God is a loving God, but isn't He also a just, righteous and holy God, too? Isn't it dangerous to proclaim a love that is perhaps too kind to sinners? Aren't we watering down the truth when we make God a pushover who welcomes *anyone?*"

We do water down God's love, but not in the way you may think. On the one hand, we water down *mercy* by shunning sinners in even the slightest degree. On the other hand, we water down *truth* by glossing over sin – even the most minor of sins. Holy Love requires *mercy* greater than we dream and takes truth farther than we dare.

Our mistake is that our picture of Holy Love is *never extreme enough.*

Here is where human love and Holy Love are worlds apart: human love stalls at both mercy for sinners as well as truth about sin, while Holy Love extends mercy and truth into mind-bending, uncomfortable, and scandalous territory.

Human love is only **modestly** compassionate. It is only **comfortably** honest. But the Holy Love of God, to adapt the old adage, uncompromisingly hates **sin** at the same time that it lavishly loves the **sinner.**

Holy Love is simultaneously completely compassionate and completely honest in the face of injustice. This tension is not a paradox, but speaks to the very nature of Holy Love. If we are ever going to love God and neighbor the way we were meant to, we must first start to stretch into this tension between unfathomable mercy and uncompromising honesty.

Undignified Absolution

"And I pray that you, being rooted and established in love, may have power, together with all the Lord's holy people, to grasp how wide and long and high and deep is the love of Christ, and to know this love that surpasses knowledge— that you may be filled to the measure of all the fullness of God."
(Ephesians 3.17a-19)

The high-resolution mercy of Christ is unfathomably wide, high, and deep. In stark contrast, the low-resolution mercy of man is pixelated, puny, and microscopic.

Human love will welcome sinners … as long as they stop sinning first.

The alcoholic is welcome – after she gets sober. Kids are welcome – as long as they behave themselves. The homeless man is welcome – as long as he takes a shower and puts on clean clothes.

Human love's embrace is reluctant and ever-conditional. But not so with the love of God. Holy Love embraces the powerless addict **before** she gets clean. This love gives her the power she can neither find in herself, nor in a counselor, nor in religion, to get clean and sober. Then, and only then, can new life truly begin. As Spencer O'Neal asserts in his marvelous book, *Spirituality and Addictions Counseling,* no counselor or religion holds the same power as the serene strength of the Spirit – the source of Holy Love. Then, as O'Neal reminds us, "With sobriety, all else is possible."

Holy Love is kind and compassionate toward unruly children, seeking to understand **why** the kids aren't alright **before** it judges them. Holy Love hugs the diseased and dirty homeless soul **before** he can get cleaned up.

If we want to love with a Holy Love, we must get past the limitations and disclaimers of human mercy. Only then can we finally embrace the broken, the beautyless, and the wounded children of God as the Father Himself has embraced them.

The Scriptures teach us, *"He sacrificed for their sins once for all when he offered himself."* (Hebrews 7.27b)

Once for **all**, the scandalous offer is extended to **every** man, woman, boy and girl, no matter how drunk, unruly, and unclean. This is the extreme **mercy** of Holy Love.

Truth We Cannot Tolerate

At the same time, Holy Love's extreme mercy makes us uncomfortable, its blunt honesty about our bad choices makes us squirm just as much.

According to 1 Corinthians 13:6, God's Holy Love does not *"rejoice at injustice, but rejoices at the truth."* Holy Love cannot tolerate a lie – indeed, Holy Love hates injustice, but rejoices in the truth. And this is the truth about everyone: we all break the same. Every man, woman, boy, and girl is a sinner.

As it is written: *"There is no one righteous, not even one; there is no one who understands; there is no one who seeks God. All have turned away, they have together become worthless; there is no one who does good, not even one."* (Romans 3.10-12, Psalm 14.1-3, Psalm 53.1-3)

"No one righteous?" the proud soul asks. "That cannot be! What about my sainted mother?"

We like to fool ourselves, but even Momma was steeped in sin.

"What about the innocent child?" we object.

There is no innocent child. Only people without exposure to children would make a claim like that.[4]

At least that's what the scriptures say – *"all have sinned and fall short."*

"That hardly seems polite," we protest.

---

4 Don't mistake understandable weakness for strength. Is a child forgivable? Of course. But innocent? Not a chance. Don't believe me? Ask your mom.

Politeness has its place, but not when it sweeps sin under the rug. Politeness, also known as excusing others, is how we should handle simple, unintended character flaws. For dealing with the intentional choice to sin, we need something much stronger. We need the truth.

This is the extreme honesty of Holy Love. Does it make us uncomfortable? It should. This is much more potent than human love. Human love overlooks sin and excuses evil because it is simply easier than speaking the truth.

Holy Love, in contrast, does not delight in candy-coating the truth, but goes right to the joint and marrow, diagnosing our broken hearts with unrestrained honesty. We may think such honesty is cold, but it is actually the greatest kind of love, the kind of love that Jesus himself demonstrated time and again.

Think about it – would a good doctor lie to you about a tumor they discovered? Or would a good friend let you continue to make a fool of yourself when you are behaving poorly? The best doctor, the best friend, and the best love are extremely honest. Even uncomfortably honest. Holy Love is more truthful than human love can tolerate.

Stretching Into the Vastness

Honesty and mercy. Mercy and honesty. I have pondered this dual nature of Holy Love for many years – mercy that is wider than I can manage, and honesty that is deeper than I can tolerate. While I have struggled to grasp these extremes, I know that nothing describes Holy Love quite as well as these two foundational principles.

I have created a simple exercise for myself to draw closer to understanding this seeming paradox of Holy Love. Like any good physical stretch, I can never quite get as far as I want, but I think this exercise gets me a little closer to understanding the Holy Love of God and its extreme mercy and truth. My prayer is that through this spiritual exercise, you might come to *"know this love that surpasses knowledge."*

Imagine all the people in the world, every soul, lined up shoulder to shoulder in order from worst to best. On one end are pedophiles and serial killers – those we would all agree are the scum of the earth. On the other end are nice children and dreamers – those we would all agree are the good people of the world.

Now Christ approaches the lineup. He starts on the far end, with the worst of the worst. The master looks the most wicked man square in the eye and says,

"You are a sinner, broken and wretched. Change your ways, for the kingdom of heaven is just a breath away."

Everyone down the line agrees with this honest assessment from the Son of God – and they even applaud such a bold word of truth.

Jesus then moves on to the next bad person and so on down the line, saying the same, honest thing:

"You are a sinner, broken and wretched. Change your ways, for the kingdom of heaven is just a breath away."

This is the extreme **honesty** of Holy Love.

At first, the rest of the people in line cannot agree more. We applaud the master with each word fitly spoken. We cheer when He tells the truth to the crooked politician, the slave trader, and the thief. Applause after applause as He speaks love's hard truth that the sin-steeped need to hear. But as He gets closer and closer to their own positions in the line, the people applaud less and less. They realize that His message is not letting up in its intensity. He says to the man who watches too much TV, the girl who lies about doing her homework, the employee who naps at his desk those same, honest words:

"You are a sinner, broken and wretched. Change your ways, for the kingdom of heaven is just a breath away."

Somewhere just left or right of center, it is your turn. He looks you in the eye and says,

"You are a sinner, broken and wretched. Change your ways, for the kingdom of heaven is just a breath away."

There is little applause from the crowd now. Just disapproving looks and disbelieving groans.

On and on down the line He goes, speaking the honest truth to each equally broken member of Adam's race. Next to the playground bully... then to the kid who snatches cookies from the cookie jar. And we get more and more uncomfortable as this love that cares enough to be honest continues toward the good end of the line. Surely someone must be good! It can't be there is no one righteous, can it? Not even **one**?

And yet, he continues on down to the very end – to a small child everyone thinks is as innocent as the dawn. Waves of anger swell down the line. Now people begin to boo Jesus. Everyone angrily protests, "Come on Jesus, not her! You call this truth? How could you be so cruel?!" Jesus has gone too far. Surely this truth is **too** honest.

But the master knows more than the crowd does – and so does the little child. He speaks those blunt words once again:

"Little one, you are a sinner, broken and wretched. Change your ways for the kingdom of heaven is just a breath away."

This is precisely what the Scriptures teach about humanity. Even the best of us is born in sin and strikes well below the mark. Where Holy Love dares to speak the truth to even the most seemingly innocent among us, surely our humanity forbids us. This love is too true, too hard, too ... **honest.**

But to stop here would only be half the exercise. The stretch is not over yet.

The master, ignoring the hissing crowd, takes the child in His arms and smiles at her, saying:

"I have always loved you and always will. Mercy is yours for the asking. Won't you receive my love and be made whole again?"

And thus begins the second part of this exercise, the stretch of mercy.

Sighs of relief are heard as the master begins to make His way back down the line, saying the same thing to the kid whole stole cookies, to the playground bully, and then to each of us.

"I have always loved you and always will. Mercy is yours for the asking. Won't you receive my love and be made whole again?"

But somewhere left of center, things begin to get dicey. One by one, He extends His embrace to more and more deplorable people. Onto the abusive father, then the pornographer, then the Auschwitz mastermind, embracing each one and saying those same, now shocking words:

"I have always loved you and always will. Mercy is yours for the asking. Won't you receive my love and be made whole again?"

He continues down the line, and none of us can stomach it anymore. We are disgusted as He looks each rapist, each cold-blooded killer, each school shooter in the eye and says those words that make the good people of the world well-up with rage.

Now nearly everyone agrees: Jesus is taking mercy too far. Surely mercy and the cross's power should not extend to this depth of wickedness and cruelty.

Still, the master continues down the line as we shake our heads in ever-growing disapproval, right to the bitter end. The second-to-last-last man in line is an amalgamation of every cruel tyrant in history – a despot a hundred times worse than Hitler, Herod, Pol Pot, and Pharaoh combined. Now we all seethe with anger as the Son of God extends his tender embrace to even this pitiful excuse for a human being.

"I have always loved you and always will. Mercy is yours for the asking. Won't you receive my love and be made whole again?"

Now the good people of the world have had enough. From their end of the line they are all – every one of them – screaming and yelling for Jesus to cease this undignified absolution. A chant arises in defiance of Christ, demanding first, "Stop! Stop!" And soon the chant changes to, "Kill! Kill!" Even the good boys and girls join the shouting, demanding an end to such a shameless display of unmerited favor.

And then their shouts turn once again from "Kill! Kill!" to "Crucify! Crucify!"

The crowd is in a rage; this mercy has gone too far. They want the Nazarene killed before He can reach the last person in line, the worst of the worst, and finish His task, once and for all.

But the master continues, His face set like flint, undeterred in His resolve. He looks at the pathetic man standing in last place, the chief of all sinners. A religious hypocrite, sick with arrogance and smug in his grotesque image of himself.

The master embraces him with arms like iron bands and says to him,

"Steve, I have always loved you and always will. Mercy is yours for the asking. Won't you receive me and be made whole again?"

We might think we understand the Holy Love of God, but when the cards are counted we really don't seem to have the stomach for it.

Holy Love from God to humanity takes both mercy and truth farther than human love ever would… or perhaps ever could. Yet this is the honesty and mercy we must show one another if we are to become true sons and daughters of God.

"Behold what manner of love the Father has bestowed on us, that we should be called children of God!" (1 John 3.1a)

"Love the Lord your God with all your heart and with all your soul and with all your strength."

(DEUTERONOMY 6.5)

PART TWO:
LOVING GOD

A Reckless Bet

In Part One, we did the hard work of considering the depth of God's Holy Love for us. We also explored just how different human love is from Holy Love.

> Where human love is reluctant, Holy Love has no limits.

> When human love just can't go on any more, Holy Love is teeming with life.

> While human love is prone to wander, Holy Love remains eternally faithful.

> Where human love falls short, Holy Love overflows.

> While human love has reasonable hesitation, Holy Love is unreasonably bold.

In short, human love is always incomplete, always withheld to a degree, and always fails. God's Holy Love for us is a reckless bettor – it is always all-in.

If you've ever doubted that God could love you in such a way, behold, once again, the cross of Jesus Christ. Stop for a moment. Give it more than a loaded half-glance. Peer into the eyes of the crucified Son of Man. What more could He have done, how much further could He have run, how much more could He have given?

There, on red tree hill, Holy Love volunteered itself, surrendered itself, completely for you and me, without reservation.

Love that Deserves a Response

Now, this all-in love deserves an all-in response. Because it is gentle and patient, Holy Love does not **demand** a response – it merely **deserves** one. And this is where we come to the big question we should always ask when we come to a new understanding of God's love:

"Now what?"

What is an appropriate response to such extravagant love from God?

Perhaps the greatest reaction we could have to God's love is to become living manifestations of this Holy Love on earth, sharing His heart, partaking in that central theme of His being. To become living vessels of Holy Love is the highest calling we could ever receive.

This is why the cross is so important to Christians. It is not the end of our faith, but the beginning. It is the means by which we can rely on Holy Love to carry us in our darkest hour. The cross is the fount from which we drink deep of Holy Love, which in turn is the source of the Holy Love we share with God and neighbor. Any version of Christianity that peddles the cross as the end-game is missing the point. Our old life ends at the cross of Jesus, and our new life starts the moment we take up our own cross to follow Him. The cross is not merely where guilt ends, it is where love – and therefore life – begins.

The cross is not the touchdown, but the kickoff.

Miss the meaning of the cross, and you will never be able to love God and neighbor aright. But see the cross of Christ as the endless source of Holy Love flowing **to** you, and therefore **through** you, and you can do all things.

And so it is no surprise that the two greatest commandments – our responses to Holy Love – according to Jesus, are to love God and to love neighbor.

The First and Greatest Response

But the greatest of the two is to love God.

"'Love the Lord your God with all your heart and with all your soul and with all your strength and with all your mind.'" (Luke 10.27)

This is a quote taken from the Hebrew Scriptures of Jesus's upbringing. It is known as the *V'ahavta,* a daily prayer recited by the Hebrew people from ancient times. It originates from Deuteronomy 6.5, *"Love the Lord your God with all your heart and with all your soul and with all your strength."*

In the next three chapters, I will address each of these dimensions of God-love in turn: heart, soul, and strength.

First, though, I need to address an issue with the Biblical text. You may notice that there is something different about the New Testament version of this verse – the word "mind" somehow got in there. Where did that come from?

No one knows exactly how, but by the time of Jesus, the original Hebrew, which used words that were very broad in meaning (as we will see very soon), had been translated into many languages as the children of Israel were exiled and dispersed throughout the ancient world through the centuries.

Since the time of Moses when they spoke Hebrew primarily, the Israelites had picked up a host of other languages and used them in daily life, including Aramaic, Greek, and probably even Babylonian, Assyrian, and Egyptian.

And what happens when you translate from one language to another? As any multilingual person can tell you, translation is rarely precise. You have to add a clarifying word here and there to round out the intent of some words – especially if the source language uses words that have a very broad range of meaning, as is the case with ancient Hebrew.

And that is exactly what happened to Deuteronomy 6.5: the Hebrew words for heart, soul, and strength are complicated, rich words with much deeper meaning than our clumsily precise English translation allows. Somewhere along the way, the scribes and rabbis before Jesus's time allowed for the word "mind" to be added to the daily *V'ahavta* prayer.

It was probably intended to expand on the Hebrew word we translate as "strength," but we're not 100% certain about that. It could just as well have been an expansion of the word we translate "soul." Or it could be that the very common Old Testament couplet "heart and soul" is echoed poetically in the phrase "mind and strength."

Fortunately, the main idea of the verse is plain: we are to love "all-in" – with everything we've got.

Heart: All You Are

The first thing we are to love with is all our heart, which I will argue means **all that we are** on the deepest level of identity.

The Hebrew word *"levav,"* which means *"heart"*, is the most literal of the three. You can practically hear a heartbeat in the sound of the word – *levav, levav, levav*. But the English word for heart has a slightly different significance than the Hebrew. In English, we use *"heart"* to talk about things like feelings ("Heartbreak Hotel") and enthusiasm ("You gotta have heart"). But the Hebrew word *"levav"* doesn't necessarily carry the same emphasis.

In Hebrew, *"levav"* refers to your **inmost** being, just as the heart is one of your most essential internal organs. To ancient Hebrews, the heart was the seat of your identity; the center of your life; the core of your being. Hebrews spoke of the heart the way we speak of the brain – you would "thinketh" in your "heart" (Proverbs 23.7, KJV) Emotions, on the other hand, were thought to reside in the gut or the kidneys – ancient Hebrew Valentines could have been stomach or kidney shaped!

So when Deuteronomy 6.5 says that we should love God with all our heart, it means that we should love God with our **inmost being.**

Soul: All You Do

The Hebrew word we translate into English as *"soul"* is *"nephesh,"* and it is one of the most complex Hebrew words with an incredibly broad range of definitions and connotations. In general, it can mean *"life"* but it can also mean *"person"* or *"spirit"* or *"state of being."*

A few examples:

In Genesis 1, the creation account, God creates sea *nephesh* (whales), then land *nephesh* (cattle and creeping things), and all the *nephesh* that fly in the air (winged fowl). Notably, in the Old Testament, plants are considered to be alive, but are not considered to be *nephesh*.

Later in Genesis 12.5, we read about Abram moving with his family and employees – his *nephesh* – from Haran to Canaan.

Nephesh is even used to refer to a corpse: that would be a "dead *nephesh*".

Now, having said all this, you can see why it is difficult to accurately explain what it means to love God with "all your *nephesh*." It is fair to say that your *nephesh* includes all that you do, but it is probably more circumspect to say that loving God with your *nephesh* means to love God with your **utmost** being; with your uttermost – or your "outermost" life. When you consider the context of *"levav"* or "heart" as referring to the **inmost** part of you, it seems fair to understand "soul" as extending outward from there to encompass **everything else** that is your life, including everything you say and do.

Strength: All You Have

And finally, we come to this other somewhat mysterious word, "You shall love the Lord your God with all your *me'od*." Again, English is too precise to capture the breadth of the meaning of the Hebrew word *me'od*, which literally means *"muchness,"* or *"abundance,"* or (perhaps too precisely) *"possessions."*

Me'od could also very fittingly be translated to mean *"wealth,"* which is exactly how it was sometimes translated in ancient Aramaic and Greek cultures. At any rate, I hope you can see that the English word *"strength"* is woefully inadequate to translate the word *"me'od"* – it might be more fitting to say, "You shall love the Lord your God with **all you have**," or, "You shall love the Lord your God with all **your stuff**."

Like many of us living in an abundant society, I have a great deal of "muchness" (or *me'od*) that I am called to love God with. This means more than simply giving to charity. It means managing and using every resource we have in the service of Holy Love.

Upcoming chapters will explore each of these three aspects of the *V'ahavta* in greater depth.

"For I will take you out of the nations; I will gather you from all the countries and bring you back into your own land. I will sprinkle clean water on you, and you will be clean; I will cleanse you from all your impurities and from all your idols.

"I will give you a new heart and put a new spirit in you; I will remove from you your heart of stone and give you a heart of flesh.

"And I will put my Spirit in you and move you to follow my decrees and be careful to keep my laws. Then you will live in the land I gave your ancestors; you will be my people, and I will be your God."

(EZEKIEL 36.24-28)

CHAPTER FIVE:

WITH ALL YOUR HEART

The Heart Specialist

I love to golf. I'm not very good at it, but I love to hit the links when I can. My mother and father instilled a love of the game in each of their six children. As an adult, I cherish any opportunity to get out on the course.

Once, I was put in a group with three other gentlemen. One of them was well past retirement age, but he still beat me on every hole. Either he was really good or I … well, I prefer to think that he was just really good. The other two men called this older man "Doc."

After a few holes, I realized I had better turn this guy into a friend before he buried me alive on the course. When Doc sent an incredible tee shot sailing straight down the middle of the fairway, I saw my opportunity.

"Are you a doctor of something besides golf?"

He turned his head, smiled and replied, "I'm a heart specialist."

"Wow!" I said, "That's a big deal. Were you a surgeon or …"

He answered, "I have dealt with every kind of heart problem you could imagine. Cold hearts, dark hearts, bleeding hearts, broken hearts …"

He saw my face turn like a screw as I tried to figure out what he was saying. There was a long pause as I tried to think of something polite to say to this obviously looney old man.

After leaving me out to dry for just a little too long he explained, "I'm a retired pastor – a Doctor of Ministry."

Although I would prefer to forget that round of golf due to my poor performance, I'm glad I met Doc. His play on words was not only entertaining to the other guys who already knew him, but also profoundly true, sticking with me to this day. In the Lord's work, every disciple must be a heart specialist.

The Bible so often uses the word "heart" to describe our deepest spiritual condition. And Doc's diagnoses of "dark hearts, cold hearts, bleeding hearts, broken hearts" – describe the spiritual human condition very well.

Joseph Conrad, in his 19th century novel *The Heart of Darkness* used the imagery of an incomplete map to describe the human heart. In the 19th century, there was a very large blank space on European maps of Africa – this "dark spot" marked out uncharted, unexplored territory – the "heart of darkness." Conrad used that idea to explore the unmapped regions of the heart. And he uncovered what the Bible teaches so clearly – that the heart of man is ultimately unsearchable and prone to desperate wickedness.

In each of our chests also beats a heart of darkness.

Pneumocardiogram

There is a type of study in medicine called a pneumocardiogram, which measures heart and lung function. For the purpose of this book I've hijacked that medical word, with apologies, and am going to use it to depict spiritual pictures of the heart – "pneumo-cardio-grams". In Greek, *"pneuma"* means *"breath"* or *"spirit,"* while *"kardia"* means *"heart,"* and *"gram"* means *"writing,"* as in written words.

The Scriptures and our language are loaded with pneumocardiograms.

In the Exodus account, we read that Pharaoh's heart was "hardened" against the Israelites. That's a spiritual word picture describing Pharaoh's soul, not his actual, physical heart.

Pop music is filled with fascinating word pictures of mankind's heart condition: Hank Williams sang about a "cheatin' heart" and Paula Abdul was, at one time, very concerned about a "cold-hearted snake."

These are all pneumocardiograms – spiritual word pictures of the human heart.

Then there is one of the of the most important pneumocardiograms in Scripture: *"wholehearted."*

We read the Lord's blessing of Caleb in the Old Testament:

*"But because my servant Caleb has a different spirit and follows me **wholeheartedly,** I will bring him into the land he went to." (Numbers 14.24a)*

We read of the leaders of Israel in the time of King David:

*"The people rejoiced at the willing response of their leaders, for they had given freely and **wholeheartedly** to the Lord. David the king also rejoiced greatly." (1 Chronicles 29.9)*

And the psalmist pleads with God:

*"May I **wholeheartedly** follow your decrees, that I may not be put to shame." (Psalm 119.80)*

It seems that anything less than wholehearted love for God is not worth the effort. The Lord is looking for those who follow Him wholeheartedly. Half-hearted love won't do. In Deuteronomy 6.5, the *V'ahavta* beckons us, *"You shall love the Lord your God will **all** your heart."*

A New Heart

This leads us to a serious problem: while the scriptures call us to love God with all our hearts, they also teach us that none of us is **capable** of loving God wholeheartedly – at least not on our own.

We have a congenital heart defect, as Jesus knew well when He walked among us. John's Gospel says *"He did not need any testimony about mankind, for he knew what was in each person." (John 2.25)*

And what was in each person? Deceit. Treachery. Or as my friend Doc would say: dark hearts, broken hearts, and bleeding hearts. Jeremiah 17.9 astutely says, *"The heart is deceitful above all things and beyond cure. Who can understand it?"*

In Ezekiel 36.25, the passage quoted at the beginning of this chapter, the Word of God takes it further and claims that we have **hearts of stone.**

And what do we know about a stone? A stone is cold, hard, and dead. There is no human campaign that can change its condition.

We might warm a cold stone in a fire, but it will eventually return to its natural state: cold. In the same way, we might temporarily warm our own hearts with happy thoughts, amusing entertainment, even a good day in church – but eventually our hearts will cool down to their original, frigid state.

By the same token, we might also try to soften a hard stone by soaking it in water but that, too, is useless. Our hearts tend to grow calloused and harder as we experience life's predictable pattern of suffering and tragedy. Evil deeds that should provoke us to action and sympathy have less and less impact over time. Another killing? Another school shooting? Let's just switch apps for a while and wait for those posts to get buried deeper in the news feed. The heart has a way of hardening itself.

And of course, a dead stone cannot be brought to life. There is nothing you or I could do to make a dead stone live. In the same way, the Scriptures say that our hearts are dead like stones. No effort of human will can ever bring a dead heart to life.

The dilemma is clear: we have hearts of stone that are incapable of loving wholeheartedly, yet God calls us to love Him "with all our hearts." If we are not able to love God "with all our heart" – with our hearts *as-they-are* – only one option remains: we need a ***new heart,*** and there is only one way to get a new heart: ***a transplant.***

"I will give them an undivided heart and put a new spirit in them; I will remove from them their heart of stone and give them a heart of flesh." (Ezekiel 11.19)

Consider the cost of the spiritual heart transplant Ezekiel proclaims. After all, this new heart of flesh has to come from somewhere, doesn't it? And just where would God get this new heart of flesh?

I once met a heart transplant recipient. I asked her what it was like to have your heart removed and a new one put in, and she told me: "It was terrifying… but I knew it had to be done. And I am so glad I did it."

Some transplants come with a higher risk than others. While a small skin graft or a corneal transplant is still very serious, a heart transplant is an all-or-nothing proposition.

I have heard of family members donating a kidney or bone marrow, but I have never heard of *any* healthy person who willingly surrendered their ***heart*** to someone else, as doing so would spell certain death.

And yet, that is what Jesus did for us. While our hearts were as cold, hard, and dead as a stone, the Son of Man – the Lord Jesus Christ – laid down His life and went under the blade.

His life for yours; His *heart* for yours.

We say things so many times that they lose their punch, but it bears repeating: the Lord has given us new life, but we must willingly receive it. Unless we accept this new heart, we cannot live. For those who refuse to receive it, the donor has given His heart in vain.

But for those who will undergo the procedure, surrender their hearts of stone, and receive the Spirit of God, a new heart is given. And with it, we are finally able to love God the way we were made to: ***wholeheartedly.***

If we want to walk in real love, we will need a new heart – the one we were born with just can't take the strain.

The good news? A Perfect Donor – Jesus Christ – is ready to remove our hearts of stone and give us a new heart that pulsates with Holy Love.

So what are you waiting for? Don't be too proud to pass His offer by. You have only to ask, and you shall receive.

Prayer for a Heart Transplant

Father, I confess to you that I have harbored a heart of stone –
I am cold when I should be hot;
I am hard when I should be tender;
I am stubborn when I should be surrendered.
Lord, take from me this heart of stone today.

Jesus, I acknowledge my need for a heart like yours –
A heart that beats aflame in the darkness;
A heart that beats alive when death surrounds me;
A heart that beats afresh with compassion for the world around me;
A heart that is warm, full of hope, and overflowing with joy.
Lord, here and now I ask: forgive me all my sin, and give me a
  heart like yours.

Holy Spirit, I ask you to breathe new life in me –
To comfort me where I am most troubled;
To trouble me where I am most comfortable;
To train and preserve this new heart that you have given me.
Lord, I ask your Spirit to guide me into all truth.

Father, Son, and Spirit: I surrender myself to your designs.
I go under your knife;
I place my heart in your hands –
And I willingly accept a new heart that will forever beat true.

Have your way in my life;
Beat strong in my heart;
Now and forevermore.

Amen!

"Love the Lord your God with all your heart and with all your soul and with all your strength."

(DEUTERONOMY 6.5)

CHAPTER SIX:
WITH ALL YOUR SOUL

We borrow many phrases from the Bible without even knowing it. Did you know "scapegoat" is lifted directly from the Bible? How about "an eye for an eye?" Those are just two of dozens of phrases we use in everyday speech that come straight from the pages of Scripture.

Another one is "heart and soul." I was always confused by that – what does that mean? Like most of us, I think I get the general idea. But what exactly does it really mean to love someone or do something with "heart and soul?"

As I said earlier, the word translated as "*soul*" in Deuteronomy 6.5 is one of those rare places where modern English translations of the Bible cannot adequately express the range of meaning of an ancient Hebrew word. In modern English, "soul" sometimes means something like "spirit." We think of a soul as departing a body at death, sort of like a ghost. But in the Bible, the word translated as "soul" as means much, much more than a ghost.

In Hebrew, the word is *"nephesh"* - which means a wide range of things. It can mean *"spirit,"* yes. But as mentioned earlier, it also can mean *"life, person, being,"* and often even *"body."* Nephesh usually seems to imply both personality – intellectual sentience – as well as physical existence.

I propose that if the Hebrew *"levav"* (*"heart"*) refers to our **inmost** being, then the Hebrew *"nephesh"* (*"soul"*) refers to everything that flows from the heart: our "**outmost"** being.

When the Bible talks about "heart and soul," it is simply talking about all of us – everything inside and out. Listen to just a few examples from Scripture where the words "heart" and "soul" appear together as a couplet – a poetic phrase meaning the whole person, inside and out:

"But if from there you seek the Lord your God, you will find him if you seek him with all your heart and with all your soul."

(Deuteronomy 4.29)

"But be very careful to keep the commandment and the law that Moses the servant of the Lord gave you: to love the Lord your God, to walk in obedience to him, to keep his commands, to hold fast to him and to serve him with all your heart and with all your soul."

(Joshua 22.5)

"Do all that you have in mind," [Jonathan's] armor-bearer said. *"Go ahead; I am with you heart and soul."*

(1 Samuel 14:7)

Even God uses the words "heart and soul" together in Jeremiah to talk about Himself:

"I will rejoice in doing them good and will assuredly plant them in this land with all my heart and soul."

(Jeremiah 32.41)

Dimensions of the Soul

I hope those selections from the Scriptures make it a bit easier to understand what it is to "love God with all your heart *(levav)* and all your soul *(nephesh)*." It means that I am committed not just somewhere deep in my heart, but also with all of my being that radiates out from it.

Many Christian groups emphasize "holiness," which means they believe that God's people are called to live differently. I believe that too. It is what the Scriptures clearly teach, from cover to cover. Those who choose to follow God are to be a holy people. Which, when you get right down to it, simply means that we are to love God "heart and soul."

But there are those in the religious world who have kidnapped the idea of "holiness" and twisted it into a cold crown of legalistic thorns, which is very far from the heart of God. They reason, *if you will just quit smoking or drinking, you will finally be holy.*

Foolishness!

To love God with all our heart and soul means more than merely the passive action of avoiding sin. Jesus said, *"What goes into someone's mouth does not defile them, but what comes out of their mouth, that is what defiles them." (Matthew 15.11)* If avoiding evil was the goal of holiness, every piece of dead wood or lifeless stone would be holy! We are made holy by the grace of God, and the grace of God alone; certainly not by our own human effort.

To review, loving God with heart and soul means pursuing what is good and right, both inside and out. It is a positive action, not a passive or negative one. (It may, however, mean that you have to leave some things behind!)

But when all is said and done, holiness is measured by the love we show God and others, heart and soul.

Let's examine three dimensions of the soul, or *nephesh*, the parts of our life that flow outward from the heart: our thoughts, our words, and our deeds.

Thoughts

Our brain is the part of our being, or *nephesh*, that has to do with our patterns of thinking. And loving God with all our soul means loving God with your methods of thinking.

"Do not conform to the pattern of this world, but be transformed by the renewing of your mind. Then you will be able to test and approve what God's will is—his good, pleasing and perfect will."

(Romans 12.2 NIV)

I love the Bible's wording – our minds conform to patterns, either of this world or of heaven. And patterns are predictable. If we conform our minds to the pattern of the news, what will the pattern be? Negative story after negative story.

If, in contrast, we pattern our minds after the Word of God, something very different will happen. God's Word reveals grace after grace, truth after truth, and love after love. Our thoughts will thus become grace after grace, truth after truth, and love after love. What patterns are we currently following? The patterns of bad news, or the pattern of the Good News?

"For as he thinketh in his heart, so is he." (Proverbs 23.7 KJV)

Words

The tongue is a very powerful two ounces of muscle.

"Likewise, the tongue is a small part of the body, but it makes great boasts. Consider what a great forest is set on fire by a small spark."

(James 3.5)

If our words flow unchecked, they can do a great deal of damage. It only takes one sentence spoken in anger to bring years of pain to a relationship. On the other hand, if our words are thoughtful, caring, and kind, they can bring life and joy and peace to the ones we love.

When the Lord calls us to love Him with all our *nephesh,* that includes the words we speak to Him and to others. Are our words kind or cruel? Harsh or healing? Are the words of our mouths acceptable in the Lord's sight?

If we want to enjoy God's fullest blessings, we will guard our words carefully.

"Let the words of my mouth and the meditation of my heart be acceptable in Thy sight, O Lord, my Strength and my Redeemer."

(Psalm 19.14 KJV)

Deeds

Finally, loving God with all our *nephesh* includes our deeds, or actions. These are the things that we do from moment to moment. Loving God heart and soul means loving Him from the very deepest part of our hearts to the very tips of our fingers. It also means loving God by serving Him with our hands and feet.

That does, indeed, mean avoiding evil. Sin, while pleasant for a season, is always destructive in the end.

"Surely wickedness burns like a fire; it consumes briers and thorns, it sets the forest thickets ablaze, so that it rolls upward in a column of smoke." (Isaiah 9.18)

But we know that avoiding sin isn't the end game. Doing **what's right** is. Do we give a ride to the widow and comfort the orphan? Do we visit the prisoner? Pray for the sick? Mend a fence? Share a sandwich? Spend a Saturday singing songs and making crafts with kids whose lives may be much more traumatic than we know?

All of these examples are ways in which we love God with our deeds. Inside and out – heart and soul.

"As the body without the spirit is dead, so faith without deeds is dead." (James 2.26)

Only By Grace

In the previous chapter we discovered that God wants to enable us to love Him **wholeheartedly** by replacing our cold hearts of stone with a heart of flesh – a heart donated joyfully by His Son, Jesus Christ. Without the heart transplant by grace through faith, none of us would be able to love God with all our hearts.

And the same is true for our souls, or *nephesh* – the rest of our being.

Without God's grace, none of us would be able to **think** according to the new pattern of Jesus.

Without God's grace and the enabling of the Holy Spirit, none of us could begin to **speak** words that bring healing and hope to the people around us.

And without the grace of Christ, we would have no motivation to **serve** God and our fellow man with our hands and feet, by doing good and caring for the practical, tangible needs of our neighbors.

May we all have the courage to surrender to the grace freely given through God's Holy Love, so that we may learn to love God with everything **we are** and everything **we do** – heart and soul.

"Love the Lord your God with all your heart and with all your soul and with all your strength."

(DEUTERONOMY 6.5)

CHAPTER SEVEN:
WITH ALL YOUR STRENGTH

With all Your "Very Much"

In the previous chapter I explained why the word "soul" is not quite adequate in most modern translations. There is also a problem with the translation of the word "strength" in this verse. The Hebrew word is *me'od,* and it is most commonly used as an adverb in Hebrew. In that form, it almost always means *"very,"* or *"abundantly"* – as in *"exceedingly."* Here are some examples from the Bible:

Sarah was ***me'od*** beautiful. (Genesis 12.14)

Abraham was ***me'od*** rich with cattle and sheep. (Genesis 13.2)

Joshua was commanded to be strong and ***me'od*** courageous. (Joshua 1.7)

The noun form of ***me'od*** is closer to *" much,"* *"excess,"* or *"abundance"* – than *"strength."*

Do you see the problem with translating that phrase: "You shall love the Lord your God with all your ... *'much'"*? A literal translation doesn't quite make sense to our ears. And so English translators of Deuteronomy 6.5, along with ancient Greeks, have often punted, translating the Hebrew *me'od* into the word *"strength."*

Interestingly, however, ancient Aramaic translators before the time of Christ used a different word: *"wealth."* "You shall love the Lord with all your wealth" seems a little closer to the idea of loving God with your abundance. But how should we translate this word – *me'od* – today?

It may help to step back for a moment and look at the overall progression in Deuteronomy 6.5 once again.

First, we are asked to love God with all our heart. In Hebrew, this is *"levav,"* or the **innermost** part of us. Second, we are love God with all our soul. In Hebrew, the word is *"nephesh,"* or the **uttermost** part of us. And third, we are to love God with all our strength. The Hebrew, *"me'od,"* is all of our much or abundance. I propose that this includes **everything that we have.**

If **heart** and **soul** are related to our identity, who we are **inside** and **out**, I believe that *me'od* is a continuation of that outward-moving arc of our being, which includes not only what **we are** and what **we do**, but also everything **we have.** In our day, a better translation might go something like this: "You shall love the Lord your God with all your **stuff.**"

Whose Stuff is it Anyway?

Do we ever have a lot of stuff! I have a garage full of boxes, and I don't even know what some of them contain. Some of us have storage units, pods, drawers, storage bins, and …

You could say that one of the hallmarks of being an American is having **too much** stuff. We never seem to be satisfied with what we have, and so we pile on more and more belongings.

Now, you can't say that simply "having stuff," as a Biblical principle, is wrong. Abraham had stuff. So did David. And more than a few other of the faithful throughout history. It isn't, in any way, wrong to simply **have** stuff.

It is, however, unChristian to have stuff that **does not belong to God** and **does not point to God.**

Belonging and Pointing to God

And that is really the test of whether we love God with all our *me'od* – our *very much,* our abundance, our *stuff* – does it all **belong** to God? And does it all **point** to God?

When I ask, "**Does it all belong to God?**" here's what I mean: if He took all of our stuff away, could we still say as Job did, "The Lord giveth and the Lord taketh away. *Blessed be the name of the Lord" KJV (Job 1.21)*? Or would we be so attached to our stuff that our true allegiance would be revealed? Maybe that's what the book of Job is really all about – where is our true allegiance? Can any of us really know until we've lost the stuff we hold most dear?

And when I ask, ***"Does it all point to God?"*** here's what I'm getting at: do we leverage what we have for the sake of His glory? If we have a home, is it all His, used to extend hospitality to those in need? Have I welcomed the alien and the stranger to my table so that they may know the love of God? Have I shared my abundance with the widow and the orphan so they can know that God has not forsaken them? If our possessions **point** to God, their primary purpose will be for the advancement of His kingdom.

Now, I'm not suggesting that we should engrave every spoon with John 3.16 or donate everything we own to charity. I am asking whether we can honestly say we have devoted everything we have, all of our belongings, to the Lord and His work.

Loving God with all our stuff means that there is no box in the garage that does not ultimately belong to Him, no sandwich we won't share with the kid who got only carrots in their lunch, no hour spent in the pursuit of wickedness, no dollar squandered on evil.

Can we say that our stuff – all of it – ultimately **belongs** to God and **points** to God? And if there are things that don't, are we willing to either surrender them to the just cause of His kingdom or divest ourselves of them? It wouldn't hurt most of us to have less stuff, to be sure. But quantity is not the issue. The real question is: do I love my stuff more than I love God?

Some may read this and think, "Ha! Gotcha there, pastor. I don't have much to begin with! I am as broke as they come! This verse does not apply to me."

Respectfully, I beg to differ. Each of us, young and old, rich and poor, has three things in abundance that make up the "stuff" we are to love God with. Each of us has ***time, treasure,*** and ***talent.***

Time

Imagine you were given full access to a bank account that accumulated exactly $1,440 each day, and your job was to spend that entire amount within 24 hours. Whatever you didn't spend would be wiped from the account at midnight. What would you spend $1,440 on?

Each day brings us the gift of 1,440 minutes. We can't get them back once they're gone. How many of those minutes *belong* to God? How many *point* to God? How are we spending the time God gives us?

When Pastor Ed Kneeland gave me a paperback New Testament on August 16, 1989 – my first personal Bible – I laughed at him. I explained to him that I was just a high school kid – there was no way I was going to read the whole Bible.

Ed wisely taught me this secret: Read a chapter a day. If you miss a day, don't sweat it. Just pick it up again the next day. Just remain open, and obedient, and His. Sure enough, within two years I had read the entire Bible, cover to cover, Genesis to Revelation. Every name. Every list. Every number. And every glorious promise. Within ten years I had read it through five more times. I know that a number of you have read it through many more times. Just a little each day day goes a very long way.

"Blessed is the one ... whose delight is in the law of the Lord, and who meditates on his law day and night." (Psalm 1:1a,2b)

Treasure

Now, let's talk about our treasure. The truth is – even for the poorest among us – we have more stuff as individuals than any other society in the history of the world. Do our belongings belong to God? Do they point people to God?

I know that many reading this have next to nothing at the end of the month once the bills are paid. But the mere act of paying our bills on time points people to God. The way we handle our treasure, large or small, illustrates the way we trust God. Christians should be the very first in our society to honor God with our finances by honoring our debts, paying our bills on time, not overextending ourselves, and – dare I suggest it? – tithing generously and cheerfully.

We love God with our stuff when we are faithful with our finances. It doesn't matter how much or little we have. Two well-managed pennies that both *belong* to and *point* to God express far greater love than a thousand bequeathed as an afterthought.

"No one can serve two masters. Either you will hate the one and love the other, or you will be devoted to the one and despise the other. You cannot serve both God and money." (Matthew 6:24)

Talent

Finally, everyone reading this has at least one talent that we can use to love God. These are your unique gifts, abilities, and skills. We all have different gifts, as Paul says, but we all must use them for the glory of God and the edification of His people and His kingdom.

Some talents are *natural.* My daughter, Cambria, is a natural-born leader and public speaker. It's just the way she was born. She is now off at college, and my prayer is that she will continue to ensure that her gifts of intelligence and a strong sense of justice both *belong* to and *point to God* as she leads a life of leadership and service to others. My son, James, is able to see the positive in almost every difficult situation. He was born with a cheerful attitude that brings comfort to many. My prayer for James is that his talent for optimism in the face of overwhelming odds both *belongs* to and *points to God* for the rest of his days. And my youngest son, John, has an innate capacity to show compassion for and include those who are less fortunate than himself. John was born with a desire to befriend those who usually end up on the margins of life. My prayer for John is that his compassionate heart will *belong* and *point to God* as he continues to show compassion for the hurting.

Some gifts, on the other hand, are *supernatural.* The Holy Spirit may have enabled you to do things that you naturally could not – or would not – do on your own. These are called spiritual gifts, and I believe that *at least one* gift is given *to every believer* for the sake of building up the body of Christ. Some are gifted as administrators. Others are gifted as teachers. Some are gifted at evangelism, prophecy, early childhood education, nursing, building, and so on. These supernatural gifts are given for the purpose of pointing others to God.

And finally, there are skills that we have **learned.** God has given each of us opportunities in life, either through experience, education, or hard work, to become skilled in a vocation or hobby. God wants you to love Him with those skills! They **belong** to Him – they should also **point** people to Him.

In the Old Testament, we read of weavers who used their talents to make the fabric walls of the sacred tabernacle in the wilderness. We have a small but dedicated brigade of "weavers" of our own in the church I belong to – BJ and Betty make Operation Christmas Child tote bags and Norma Jean sews "Jesus Quilts" by the hundreds. Some folks can grill. Some can drive. Some can teach. Some can play musical instruments. Others can build with wood, steel, and stucco. But all of us can love God with our talents, remembering that these talents are meant to **belong to God** and **point people to God.**

"For we are God's handiwork, created in Christ Jesus to do good works, which God prepared in advance for us to do." (Ephesians 2:10)

PART THREE:
LOVING NEIGHBOR

Summiting Everest

If you've skipped ahead to this point, I must warn you: go back and read Parts One and Two first, or Part Three will be meaningless to you.

There are no quick answers for a failing marriage. There are no easy tips for transforming our enemies into friends. The only thing that can alter the narrative of broken human relationships is Holy Love.

To skip ahead to this part of the book without first doing the groundwork of developing your sense of both *being loved by God* and *loving God* would be a deadly mistake.

Each year, many adventurers attempt to climb Mt. Everest, the highest mountain on earth. Only a few actually make it – and many of them die on Nepal's icy slopes. Because of the dangers to both climbers and rescuers, every daring soul who wishes to climb Everest is required to spend several days at a base camp far below the summit. Why? They must acclimate their lungs and bodies to the elusive and precious thin air at those soaring heights.

More important than having the right gear, clothing, and provisions, a climber needs to first learn to breathe the new air at that incredible altitude.

Their body must be transformed at every level to the new atmosphere. Their lungs, heart – even their cells – must undergo a transformation in order to be able to process oxygen out of the thin atmosphere.

In short, an Everest mountaineer **must learn to breathe all over again** or they will not survive.

By the same token, those of us who want to see love come true in our earthly relationships must first spend the time needed to acclimate to the atmosphere of Holy Love. As we breathe in the air of Holy Love from God *for* us, then exhale the air of Holy Love **given back** to God, our souls become acclimated to a completely new way of loving and being loved. This new breath of Holy Love is the only way to tread the risky slopes of human love successfully.

If we have done the hard work of acclimating to Holy Love in Parts One and Two, then we are ready to proceed! Let's begin our ascent.

Holy Love's Third Dimension

Three times outside the gospels, the New Testament writers were inspired by the Holy Spirit to remind us of the importance of loving others, directly quoting from Leviticus 19.18 – *"Love your neighbor as yourself."* (Once in Romans 13:9, again in Galatians 5.14, and one final time in James 2.8).

This principle must be very important for it to be restated time, and time, and time again!

In each instance, we are sharply reminded that Jesus takes no delight in a legalistic approach to obeying the law. Rather, He beckons us to mirror His example, expressing love rather than avoiding hate.

When we focus on avoiding the elements that contradict Holy Love – limits, intolerance, conditions – we lose focus on the true task of loving one another. To truly experience Holy Love, we must focus on exactly what that *is*, not what it *is not*. Holy Love is conditionless, limitless, merciful, truthful and raw. We should aim to love this way rather than aiming to avoid *not* loving this way. In other words, try to hit a homerun rather than trying *not* to strike out.

Keeping the law is not love any more than not hitting fouls is how to win a baseball game. You could hit nothing but fair balls and never score a single run. Similarly, simply not murdering our neighbor doesn't mean that we love them.

This is why the **law** is powerless, and **grace** is all-powerful. Keeping the law never made a life worth living, any more than avoiding fouls won a World Series. Winners in the game of life have taken their eyes off of the foul line of the law, off of rules and regulations, and focused on the game-winning strategy of love.

Doing No Harm, Serving, and Showing Mercy

Returning to the three New Testament passages where *"Love your neighbor as yourself"* appears, it is important to note that each one is subtly nuanced and reveals a varied shade of meaning related to the high calling.

First, in Romans 13:9, Paul emphasizes that love **does no harm** to our neighbor.

Then, in Galatians 5:14, Paul emphasizes that love **serves** our neighbor.

Finally, James 2:8 reveals that love **shows mercy** to our neighbor.

As we study these three passages in the chapters to come, we will see a trajectory emerge – that loving our neighbor begins with doing no harm, extending to serving others, and, finally, showing mercy to those around us.

Let no debt remain outstanding, except the continuing debt to love one another, for whoever loves others has fulfilled the law.

"The commandments, 'You shall not commit adultery,' 'You shall not murder,' 'You shall not steal,' 'You shall not covet,' and whatever other command there may be, are summed up in this one command: 'Love your neighbor as yourself.'

"Love does no harm to a neighbor. Therefore love is the fulfillment of the law."

(ROMANS 13:8-10)

CHAPTER EIGHT:
LOVE DOES NO HARM

Contrary to what we may have heard or experienced, love is the key concept of the Christian faith. If we want to understand Jesus, we need to understand this: *love comes first.*

Love is the one vital sign that the Holy Spirit is constantly monitoring. Not our giving or our good deeds; not our Bible knowledge or our lofty prayers. God desires one quality in us above all else: Holy Love.

We have one job to do as followers of Jesus, and that is to love. God first, and each other second. I fear that many modern churches have abandoned these primary commands and instead chased after church growth paradigms that sound more like marketing strategies than a Gospel of Holy Love.

What good is it to attract crowds like moths to our entertaining but loveless shows – excuse me, "services" – as if the Tonight Show is the model we should be matching? We're winning converts to show business, not the love of God. When we win people *to* or *through* anything besides love for God and neighbor, we make them twice as much sons and daughters of hell as when they first started.

The body of Christ has one job – to love. Everything else we do must either serve that goal or be abandoned.

The Unpayable Debt

Most of us struggle with financial debts. Whether a car payment, a credit card, or a mortgage, we all feel the sting. However, there are other kinds of debt. I can owe someone a shift at work, or a weekend helping them move.

But according to the Bible, there's an even bigger debt we all owe one another: the debt to love. In fact, as the Scriptures lay it out, it's the biggest debt you and I will ever have. We might pay off all our loans and mortgages, all our favors to friends, every credit card, but we will never pay in full what we owe when it comes to love.

There is no amount of love we can pay forward that will cover the bill Jesus Christ paid on the cross for our sins. We owe Him – big time. His love is so rich, and so extravagant, and so generous, that if we wanted to write it out as a bill to be repaid, there wouldn't be enough receipt tape in the world.

And yet, peculiarly, with this debt, the more we pay, the more we gain. The more love you show, the more you get back from others. You lose nothing by loving another person; you gain everything. To pay your debt of love for your neighbor is really to enrich yourself, for one of the few things we can "take with us" is our relationships.

"Let no debt remain outstanding, except the continuing debt to love one another, for whoever loves others has fulfilled the law." (Romans 13:8)

Love Does No Harm

As with anything, there must be boundaries to alert us when we go off track. The most famous list of boundaries in the Bible is the Ten Commandments. The first part of the Ten Commandments tells us how to love God. The second part, known as the second table of the law, spells out how **not to harm our neighbor.** Thou shalt not steal, thou shalt not kill, thou shalt not covet thy neighbor's wife, etc.

"Thou shalt **not** ..."

The law tells us how not to harm our neighbor.

If you look closely, there is a fascinating progression in the second table of the law, starting by listing foul deeds (stealing, killing, adultery), then progressing to foul words (bearing false witness), and finally to foul thoughts (coveting your neighbor's spouse and belongings).

Let's take a closer look at that natural trajectory.

A Love that Expels

We know that love is patient, and love is kind, but love is also **expulsive.** In other words, love **expels** and **excludes** certain things from our list of approved behavior. These are foul balls that are the opposite of love; things that harm our neighbor.

What are the fouls when it comes to loving our neighbor as ourselves?

Harmful Deeds

Let's start with the easiest to identify: **harmful deeds.**

Thou shalt not steal, or kill, or kick puppies. These are obvious fouls, and it doesn't take a lot of reasoning to persuade anyone that these behaviors are the enemies of Holy Love. For this reason, we should all give careful thought to our conduct – the way we treat people is how we put on the clothes of the Gospel. How we love others might well be measured by how far we go out of our way to avoid harming them!

Harmful Words

Next comes one foul that I think most of us would agree on but is rampant today in some contexts (particularly on social media): **harmful words.**

Gossip, putting others down, shaming, ranting, roasting…. All of these are fouls. Sadly, I have seen every one of these sins abundantly in the church. It doesn't matter if our "observations" are correct – listing them is harmful as they're not from God or pointing to God. People don't care what we know until they know that we care. We cannot shame someone with our words and love them at the same time. We will be held accountable for every harmful word we've written or spoken.

"Do not let any unwholesome talk come out of your mouths, but only what is helpful for building others up according to their needs, that it may benefit those who listen." (Ephesians 4:29)

"Anyone who says to a brother or sister, 'Raca,' is answerable to the court. And anyone who says, 'You fool!' will be in danger of the fire of hell." (Matthew 5:22b)

Harmful Thoughts

Finally, we come to the heart of doing no harm to our neighbor: *harmful thoughts.* This is the most important truth, because all of our words and deeds flow from one source: our thoughts. In other words, if we allow ourselves to entertain harmful thoughts about a neighbor, we have sinned. Jesus said that whoever looks at a girl with lust in his eye has committed adultery and done harm to himself. The Bible teaches us to take every thought captive. Why? Because there is a progression when it comes to sin – first we *think* something, then we *say* or *act* upon it.

It is only natural to think bad thoughts, but we are called to be supernatural – to rise above our flesh and walk in the Spirit. And for those who walk in the Spirit, the harmful thoughts of malice, envy, lust, greed, and so on have no place. Loving our neighbor means giving no harbor to harmful thoughts against him.

2 Corinthians 10:5 says, "*We demolish arguments and every pretension that sets itself up against the knowledge of God, and we take captive every thought to make it obedient to Christ.*"

Beyond Morality

Some may read this and conclude that I am a mere moralist. In other words, that I am equating the deep inner impulses of Holy Love with nothing more than prudish behavior. Nothing could be farther from the truth.

While it is possible to mimic external morality for a time without the abiding internal impetus of Holy Love, such morality will always be short-lived. Why? Because it is imposed from the outside, and does not explode from within.

If we desire to truly love, and therefore become truly moral, we must go beyond the superficial exercise of merley restraining external ill behavior and develop a heart that is saturated in the ways of Holy Love.

Only when we internalize the power of this higher, Holy Love will we be able to rise above our animal instincts and demonstrate true love for our neighbor.

At its most basic level, Holy Love does no harm.

"For you were called to freedom, brothers.
Only do not use your freedom as an opportunity
for the flesh, but through love serve one another.
For the whole law is fulfilled in one word: 'You shall love your
neighbor as yourself.'

But if you bite and devour one
another, watch out that
you are not consumed
by one another."

(GALATIANS 5:13-15)

CHAPTER NINE:
FREE TO SERVE

G alatians 5:14 implores us to serve others. Specifically, we are challenged with this mandate: "through love, serve one another."

Before we can talk about the high road of serving our neighbor, Paul wants to remind us of the dangerous low road of serving ourselves. In verse 13 he says, *"...do not use your freedom as an opportunity for the flesh ... "*

Selfish Slavery

Without the context of the rest of Paul's fiery letter to the Galatians, it is tough to see what he was getting at. Paul was talking about the fact that in Christ we are free from religion and legalism – and all the rules and regulations that come with them.

At the time of his writing, there was a roiling fight among Christians in Galatia over whether people who were part of this new movement of Jesus the Nazarene needed to follow the Old Testament Jewish ceremonial law. Of particular concern to the people of Paul's day was the issue of circumcision. Every God-fearing Jewish male was circumcised according to ceremonial law. But most new Greek converts, especially those in Galatia, had understandable reservations about getting circumcised.

The Jewish Galatian followers of Jesus were asking, "Should we require our new Greek brothers in Christ to be circumcised? Or is it enough to tell them to love God and neighbor?"

Paul comes down forcefully on the side of grace, saying that in Jesus Christ we have been freed from legalism, and set free to do what is right. In Jesus Christ, Paul argues, the only thing that matters is grace working itself out in love for God and neighbor. Forget about circumcision!

But there was a problem with claiming the law – "the foul line" – doesn't have power anymore. Paul was worried that some people might misunderstand him. They might have believed he was saying that since the law is powerless for those who walk in forgiveness through the cross, that "anything goes."

In other words, since the head coach, Jesus, has basically said, "Forget about the foul line. Don't focus on the foul line anymore. Focus on hitting home runs," some people might get the wrong impression and think it is all right to intentionally hit fouls.

In today's context, a novice Christian might say, "If the law is powerless in Christ, then I'm going to go out and commit adultery." Or "I'm going to go out and steal." Or covet. Or kill.

Paul says, emphatically, "No, no, *no!*" Yes, we are free from the tyranny of focusing on the foul line, but we are free from it *so that we can hit home runs.* We are free to *focus on doing the right things;* not free to hit intentional fouls and see just how awful we can be.

You and I were set free for a reason: to love others by serving them, and not to indulge ourselves by doing whatever we please. The law is powerless over us, but not irrelevant, says Paul. A foul is still a foul. Sin is still sin.

Jesus didn't come to abolish the foul lines, but to fulfill the righteous requirement of God by empowering us to knock it out of the park in love.

And that is the point of verse 13. Paul desperately warns those of us who walk in the light of forgiveness to avoid the hellish sinkhole of selfishness. Selfishness – serving self above all others – is a devouring evil. Selfishness is the opposite of service to others. It wants to hit every foul it can. It is a vortex, a pit of quicksand, always hungry for more, always aching to fill our unfillable bellies in the name of self-preservation.

Self-serving drains life from the Body of Christ as it seeks to find fulfillment in pursuing the desires of the flesh. The way of Jesus Christ, and therefore the way of Holy Love, is the way of freedom found in **serving others.**

Selfless Freedom

Paul goes on to say at the end of verse 13, *"...but through love serve one another."*

Paul says that to love our neighbor as ourselves means to serve them. In contrast to the sinkhole of selfishness, he urges us to seek the selfless spring of service to others – in love. This is the noble, God-honoring life that brings joy: serving one another.

Whether it is by helping a neighbor with a practical need, or listening to a friend in tears through the night, we exemplify Holy Love when we serve others. It is evidence of an overflowing, fulfilled, and secure life in Christ. Like a fountain that never runs dry, our lives will constantly overflow in sacrificial love for others when we are supplied by God's Holy Love.

Serving: The Measure of Love

Now, we come to that pivotal verse:

"For the whole law is fulfilled in one word: 'You shall love your neighbor as yourself.'" (v14)

In other words, you and I have a mandate to serve others the way we want to be served. Or, as Jesus puts it in Matthew 7:12, *"do to others as you would have them do to you."*

In every situation, we should be thinking, "How would I want to be treated if I were in that other person's shoes?"

"If I needed a job, would I want someone to recommend me?"

"If I needed to get the grocery shopping done, would I want someone to watch my kids for an hour?"

Whom Should I Serve?

Jesus warns us against serving only those we **like** or **find agreeable.** In fact, the message of the Good Samaritan story is that our neighbor includes even those we might usually consider our enemies, whether personally or politically.

This is not something that comes naturally to human beings, especially when our wings are clipped by the limitations of weak, human, and unholy love. Yet all-powerful, divine, Holy Love – working through us by the power of the Holy Spirit – makes loving our enemies not only possible, but ultimately *inescapable.*

When we have been truly caught by Holy Love – the love that gave its life for us while we were sworn enemies of God – that same love wells up inside and cannot help but spill over into serving even our most despised enemies. The measuring cup I use *as I serve my enemy* is the same one God will use to measure out His blessings to me.

Dying of Consumption

Finally, in verse 15, Pauls echoes what he expressed in Romans 13:9, and adds on a reminder once again that love *does no harm:*

"But if you bite and devour one another, watch out that you are not consumed by one another." (v15)

In every recent election cycle we have been able to see very plainly the way that stubborn pride and political selfishness – on both sides – is able to not only divide, but devour and emaciate the family of God.

Jesus is neither Republican nor Democrat. Both the Christian right and the Christian left are broken, and neither is perfect. Jesus Christ is King of kings and Lord of lords. On some issues He is more conservative than we may be comfortable with. Other issues, He is more liberal than we can stomach. We answer to Christ alone, and we must never bow unquestioningly to the siren songs of any political party. For the sake of Heaven's Kingdom, we must serve one another in the name of Holy Love.

Beyond the scope of politics, there is no shortage of opportunities to serve those we disagree with. Whatever man made factions divide us – whether race or religion, nationality or neighborhood – Holy Love compels us to serve one another – *everyone* – as neighbors.

"If you really keep the royal law found in Scripture, 'Love your neighbor as yourself,' you are doing right. But if you show favoritism, you sin and are convicted by the law as lawbreakers."

"Speak and act as those who are going to be judged by the law that gives freedom, because judgment without mercy will be shown to anyone who has not been merciful. Mercy triumphs over judgment."

(JAMES 2.8-9,12-13)

"Then the master called the servant in. "'You wicked servant,' he said, 'I canceled all that debt of yours because you begged me to. Shouldn't you have had mercy on your fellow servant just as I had on you?'"

(MATTHEW 18.21-35)

CHAPTER TEN:
MERCY'S TRIUMPH

L *es Miserables* is, in many ways, the good news according to Victor
Hugo – a sweeping tale of mercy's triumph over judgment.

Early in the novel, the main character, Jean Valjean, escapes from prison
and while on the lam is taken in as a guest of a frail but kindly bishop who
knows nothing about Valjean's hardened past.

During supper with the bishop, a ravenous Valjean ogles the valuable
silver table settings – taking special note of two expensive and very precious
candlesticks. His lustful eye does not escape the bishop, who opts to say
nothing.

After supper, the bishop retires, leaving Valjean to wrestle with his
conscience. Eventually, in the middle of the night Valjean can no longer
resist his impulses and ransacks the dining room, making off with all the
silver – except for the two candlesticks. Even as he commits his dastardly
crime against the kindly old bishop, Valjean cannot bring himself to steal
such precious treasures.

Valjean doesn't get far, however – a watchful constable nabs him as soon
as he leaves the bishop's home. Valjean is caught red-handed clutching a
bag brimming with stolen loot. Now a true criminal, he lies to the constable, telling him, laughably, that the bishop had given the precious silver to

him as a gift. The lawman sees through Valjean's pathetic story and wakes the bishop to expose Valjean's ridiculous claim.

By all accounts, Valjean is finished at this point. The bishop will surely expose Valjean's lie and pronounce judgment – and Valjean will be taken back to prison for the rest of his miserable life.

However, in a pivotal plot twist, the bishop hears Valjean's phony story – an obvious lie – then takes the precious candlesticks from the table, hands them to Valjean, and says (to paraphrase), "My friend, you left so quickly with those other gifts that you forgot to take the best – these candlesticks."

Both the constable and Valjean are gobsmacked. The constable tries to argue with the old man, but the bishop insists and dismisses the constable.

When the man of law is finally gone, it is just the saintly old man and the hardened criminal in the room together. The bishop says to an ashamed Valjean, "I have bought your soul for God. You must use this treasure to become an honest man."

Valjean hurries off into the night, stunned by what has happened to him. He experiences several days of inner turmoil over the bishop's mercy he did not deserve, but ultimately he comes to his knees and surrenders himself to God. From that point on, Valjean becomes a new man, serving God and the cause of mercy. When Valjean dies old and full of years, the two candlesticks are on the mantle next to his bed, reminders of the mercy that forever changed his life.

When mercy triumphs over judgment, villains become heroes.

Mercy is the Message

If Paul (formerly known as the villain Saul) teaches us in Romans 13.9 that love for neighbor **does no harm** to a neighbor, and in Galatians 5.14 goes on to instruct us that love for neighbor **serves** that neighbor in their time of need, then in James 2.8, we discover the noblest and most potent manifestation of love for neighbor: **showing mercy.**

Mercy is at the very heart of Jesus's mission. His purpose was not merely to **show mercy to us**, but also to teach us how to **show mercy to our neighbor.** His mercy for us is the pattern we must follow with those around us. Being merciful is not a suggestion; it is not optional for a disciple.

The opposite of mercy is judgment – something we all know too much about. Even though each of us has been on the receiving end of judgment, we are remarkably content to judge others. As much as we cry foul when we see someone else judging another, we fiercely reserve our own "right" to judge our neighbor when they have done us wrong.

We justify our judgment by reciting legal precedent – chapter and verse; the letter of the law. And who can argue with the hard evidence that real life reveals? One doesn't have to look hard to find abundant reason to judge our neighbor. The question isn't **whether** our neighbor will stumble so that we can judge them, but **when.**

Of course that man is a cheater – at heart, every man is. Of course that woman is a gossip – at heart, every woman is. Of course Valjean is a thief – at heart, **we all are.** If we look for even one reason to justify judging our neighbor, we will discover ten thousand.

But the problem is that judgment is the least potent, least effective, response to injustice. Why? Because judgment does not change people. Judgment ultimately begets shame and pain and therefore contributes to more injustice. Only one person has the right to judge another human being, and thankfully, He is far more patient than either you or me!

Mercy, however, gently lays a wrench in gears of judgment, sabotaging the law of sin and death with the new law of mercy and grace. Mercy upends the machinery of human love's pathetic demand of eyes for eyes and teeth for teeth. Mercy, like the bishop in *Les Miserables*, taps into the transformational, life-changing power of Holy Love by turning the other cheek and forgiving those who know not what they do.

Judgment is the very lowest positive response we can give in the face of injustice. Judgment may restrain evil, but it cannot convert evil to good. Judgement, no matter how practical and justified, is always weaker than mercy for this very reason. Judgment may stop a criminal from committing further offenses, but it cannot change his direction. Mercy, however, moves jagged mountain hearts. Judgment may stop the bleeding, but it does not heal the wounded heart. Where judgment restrains and shames our neighbor, mercy restores and saves her.

Dr. Martin Luther King wrote, "Darkness cannot drive out darkness; only light can do that. Hate cannot drive out hate; only love can do that."

Judgment cannot drive out injustice. Only mercy can do that. Judgment serves a societal purpose by *restraining* the hands of the wicked, but mercy serves the higher spiritual purpose by *retraining* their hearts.

If we are to be a people of Holy Love, we must follow the path of Christ and trade the prison yard of judging our neighbor for the rehabilitation grounds of mercy. We cannot love as God loves us if we selectively judge one another. We can only love as God loves if we opt for mercy when we are faced with the opportunity to judge our neighbor.

Partiality and Prejudice

The root cause of our desire to cling to judgment instead of mercy, according to James, is favoritism, or *partiality.* In other words, giving preference to one person over another *for any reason.* James uses the example of rich and poor in the beginning of James 2, but he could just as well have used any example where we are given to partiality.

For example, James could have decried favoritism based on race, political affiliation, age, education – or even spiritual maturity, for that matter.

The principle remains the same: no one is *less* important than anyone else. In Holy Love, the small child matters no less than the adult; the questioning heart matters no less than the settled one; an immature soul in Christ matters no less than a seasoned disciple. In Christ, my enemy is no less important to God than I am.

James goes on to teach us that mercy is the opposite of prejudice. The two are mutually exclusive. Where there is mercy, prejudice cannot exist; where there is prejudice James insists that *mercy will be withheld.*

Nothing poisons a relationship as efficiently and painfully as prejudice. Prejudice is a masterful killer. The pathology of prejudice is always the same: certain, slow spiritual death.

As long as even one person among us thinks they deserve mercy more than any other, every relationship is contaminated. The call to Holy Love demands is that we remain vigilant against prejudice of all kinds.

This is especially true for those who are part of the Body of Christ, the church. Jesus himself consistently teaches that as long we find ourselves unwilling to show mercy to even one person, God's mercy will remain out of reach.[5] And who could know more about mercy than the Crucified One?

"Father, forgive them," He said as they pounded spikes into His hands. There He was, vulnerable by choice, strapped naked to a pointed and splitting timber. He had every reason to withhold mercy, every right to vent pure wrath on His oppressors. But Jesus Christ chose to offer mercy to His enemies – not retribution.

You and I were the enemies that day. You pinned His bloody arms down while I swung the sledge. If there was ever a reason to show partiality toward us, it was then. Yet, while we toiled against Him in judgment without mercy, He withheld His judgment and showed only mercy to us.

Mercy's Measure

James reminds us that mercy triumphs over judgment. That is the good news: **God's** mercy triumphed over **His** judgment of us. But the story is meant to continue: does **our** mercy triumph over **our** judgment of our neighbor?

Just as we cannot earn **God's mercy,** neither do we have any right to demand that our neighbor earn **our mercy.** A careful reading of the Gospels reveals that Jesus will not measure mercy to us according to our **best effort,** our **average**, or even our **best out of ten,** but according to our **lowest score.**

He didn't say, "With the measure you use **with those that are easy to forgive,** it will be measured to you." The implication is that my stingiest extension of mercy toward my neighbor will serve as the measure He uses with me.

Of course, this raises a very practical question: just how far should we take mercy? Is there a point when we take mercy too far? How do we know when to stop being merciful? Won't we be fools if we keep showing mercy to those who don't appreciate it?

If showing mercy made us fools, Christ on the cross would be the greatest fool of all. As the Scriptures say:

"We love because **He first loved us.**" (1 John 4.19)

---

5 Read *The Parable of the Unjust Steward* (Luke 16.1-13)

Bandwidth and Throughput

This precept of mercy for mercy, even though it is abundantly attested to in the Scriptures, creates a serious problem for a theology based on salvation by grace through faith alone. It sounds suspiciously like a works-based system of salvation. "Mercy for mercy" sounds disturbingly close to "eye for eye" and "tooth for tooth."

But a closer look reveals that requiring mercy is not the same as requiring works. Mercy is relenting from vengeance, whereas eye for eye is relenting from mercy. Indeed, eye for eye is precisely the unholy work of vengeance.

So then, what should we do with Jesus's clear instruction that *showing* mercy is required to *receive* mercy? Which comes first: the mercy we receive from God or the mercy we show to others?

Unlike the chicken and egg scenario, we know which comes first – mercy from God, expressed through Jesus' atoning death on the cross. Whatever mercy we might show is a response. It is *subsequent* to salvation. It comes *after.*

This movement of mercy – mercy's flow – can be likened to "throughput." In other words, the capacity of *mercy inward* might be limited only by the flow of *mercy outward.* The more we allow mercy to flow through our lives and fill the lives of others, the more abundantly it will flow into our own lives again.

In good faith, the Father has primed the pump and filled our cups to overflowing through His atoning death and resurrection. As long as His Holy Love overflows through us into expressions of mercy toward others, we will continue to *grow in our capacity* to show mercy.

But, on the other hand, if we refuse to overflow abundantly in mercy toward others, we have given the mercy we receive every reason to cease. The water that was once alive in us becomes stagnant because it has nowhere to flow. Mercy received but not shared is the perfect picture of spiritual death.

The Dead Sea is dead because it has no outlet. Water goes in, but none comes out. In contrast, the Sea of Galilee to the north teems with life because the water that enters it flows out to the Jordan River. The words of Christ are clear: only when we share the mercy we have received from God with our neighbor can we experience the fullness of God's Holy Love.

A Higher Precedent: The Royal Law

James describes the command to "love your neighbor as yourself" as "the royal law." We may think that he's implying the law is, for lack of a better word, "snazzy." To Americans like me, anything "royal" seems upscale and fancy – it stirs thoughts of British accents and Buckingham palace.

But that's not what James is talking about.

In ancient times, a royal law was a decree from the king that overruled every other law. It was the king's word, and it outclassed every other legal precedent.

And so when James calls "love your neighbor as yourself" the "royal law," he means that all other laws take a back seat to this one. The law of love and mercy overrules the law of retribution and revenge, of partiality and prejudice.

It's tragic, but true: prejudice always has its reasons. A parent might have very good reasons to assume his son is up to no good when he's gotten in trouble before. Prejudgment is usually based on a precedent. We almost always have a reason to resort to prejudice instead of mercy.

But may I suggest that mercy has a much higher precedent than any of our reasons for prejudice?

Once again, at the cross, the royal law – the royal decree of the King of kings – overrules all of our petty human arguments against showing mercy to our wayward child, husband, or wife. How can we bask in the mercy of the crucified Son of God and at the same time deny mercy to our neighbor?

In the courtroom where we were acquitted of all wrongdoing by Christ's mercy, is there any argument based on prejudice that our highest judge and King could possibly consider valid? Were we not all traitors and assassins – felons against every rule of God?

There are no misdemeanor sins. Like a plate of perfect glass, God's law is a gleaming, singular entity. To break one part is to ruin the whole thing. As James says, to show contempt for any portion of the law is to show contempt for it all. Therefore, we are all culpable of tainting it. And yet, when our conviction was sealed – when He had every reason to condemn each one of us – *He showed us mercy.*

And so we must treat each other if we wish to honor the conditions of our own pardon.

Disclaimer

Before finishing this chapter, I need to address mercy from a societal perspective. Although it is true that mercy transforms the heart while consequences merely restrain the hands, those who are in positions of authority (judges, parents, employers) have an obligation to restrain evil that sometimes necessitates withholding mercy from those under their jurisdiction.

An employer, for example, has an obligation to the entire company to do what is fair and just, and sometimes that may not leave them the option of showing mercy to an employee who does not do their work. By the same token, a judge has an obligation to their entire community to do what is fair and just, and that includes handing down real sentences on those who are found guilty of a crime. Parents, too, have an obligation to their entire family to do what is fair and just for everyone when one child harms another.

Being merciful on a personal level does not excuse those of us in authority from exercising justice on a societal level, be that family, company, community, or even country. When we have been entrusted by others to oversee the restraint of evil, we have an obligation to deal in consequences rather than mercy.

Even so, there may be times when showing mercy in such a situation may be allowable – and even benefit both the offender as well as society. In such cases – and perhaps always when making tough calls – it may be wise to err on the side of mercy.

Mercy First

Without a doubt, Holy Love demands *morality* ("doing no harm to our neighbor").

And Holy Love also requires that we *do good deeds* ("serving our neighbor").

But most important to the cause of Holy Love is that we *extend mercy to our neighbor.*

Why is mercy most important?

Because God's mercy covers our own debts. Mercy forgives our moral failings and our apathy in serving others. Mercy is always the victor, because mercy, proven at the cross, is the only solid ground we have ever had to stand on.

Personal morality does not triumph over judgment. Outward good deeds and acts of service do not triumph over judgment. These feats of human effort are too feeble and imperfect. The only ethical value that supersedes judgment is mercy. It is all we have, and all we can claim.

Only when we become people of mercy will we begin to see our relationships with one another bloom into peace. Holy Love – the love that never fails – is, above all, abundant in mercy.

May the same be said of us!

"Blessed are the merciful, for they will be shown mercy." (Matthew 5.7)

CHAPTER ELEVEN:

MARKDOWN MERCIES

In spite of the fact that mercy is extreme – far more extreme than we are comfortable with – we sometimes manipulate mercy until it becomes something less. I call this "false mercy."

False mercy usually masquerades sanctimoniously as "forgiveness," but in the end it turns out to be the opposite of loving our neighbor.

For example, mercy that constantly covers-up a child's unexplained injuries – thus enabling an abusive parent to continue in sin – cannot be genuine mercy. Even though words that go along with mercy may be used ("I forgive you"), *mercy that enables injustice is a lie.* Covering up abuse – and therefore excusing injustice – is the polar opposite of Holy Love, for Holy Love gives no harbor to injustice.

False mercy is no mercy at all; it stands in the way of transformation and redemption in our relationships – whether among our immediate neighbors, or in society as a whole. Until we walk in true mercy, we will have no peace – either at home or on earth.

It is absolutely essential that we learn to identify false mercies so that we can exhibit genuine mercy. The following three examples are just a few of the many imposters that may appear to be mercy. These false mercies often use the same words and expressions as legitimate mercy – but they are really only shadows of the truth.

Mistimed Mercy

Timing is everything, especially when it comes to showing mercy – and true mercy can only properly be given *after* an offense is acknowledged. If we show mercy too early, it simply doesn't make sense. More than that, mistimed mercy loses its effective power.

Mistimed mercy is mercy that is given prematurely. Mercy makes sense only *after* an offense is exposed and acknowledged for what it is. When we offer mercy before acknowledging that something was done wrong we cheapen it, lessening its value.

Think of mercy as paying a dinner bill. If my friend and I go out to dinner, and he offers to pay the bill after we've eaten, that has great value!

But if my friend attempts to pay the bill before we've ordered anything, it means nothing because we don't owe anything. You can't pay for dinner until you've gotten the check. Where there is no accounting, there is no price to be paid. And where there is no price to be paid, there is no value.

Mercy can only come *after* there has been a proper accounting of sin and the offending party is clearly shown to be a debtor. Mercy is only meaningful after the bill has been tallied and laid on the table.

So what does this look like in relation to our neighbors – friends, family or otherwise?

For starters, it means we need to be honest with those who have harmed us in word or deed before we begin to talk about mercy. We need to acknowledge their offenses (and be open to the fact that we may have committed some ourselves!) before we can consider taking the brave step of offering forgiveness.

In other words, genuine mercy is brutally honest about sin. Real mercy never sweeps sin under the rug.

We see this misappropriation of mercy play out all too often in abusive relationships. How many wives are tragically quick to forgive their husbands without first acknowledging the terrible consequences and the deep hurt they have caused? In an effort to keep the peace by sweeping abuse under the rug, these well-meaning sisters are inevitably prolonging everyone's pain. Abusive husbands must have their sins exposed and acknowledged, and they must face the real consequences of their actions before mercy can have any meaning at all in their minds.

Of course, I appreciate that the example I've just given is hopelessly simplistic. Escaping from an abusive relationship is far easier said than done, and rehabilitation requires a circle of accountability for both the abused and the abuser. However, I hope even this meager example helps to illustrate the point that mercy given prematurely is not the same kind of mercy rendered by Holy Love. Genuine mercy may only properly be applied after a guilty verdict has been reached.

How about a more personal, spiritual example?

For those of us who rely on the mercy of God through the cross of Jesus, we know that confession is the pivotal moment when mercy becomes real in our hearts. Whether it is reciting the sinner's prayer for the first time or kneeling in a confessional, we recognize that mercy is actualized only *after* we acknowledge our need for it.

Again, this is another reason why I am not a universalist. It would be downright rude of God to force mercy on those who don't want it. Yet when the time comes when we are finally busted, mercy means everything.

In personal terms, this means that we have an obligation to help an offending brother see the error of his ways before we adorn him with laurels of cheap mercy. This should be done in proper order, as Jesus taught us with Matthew 18.

First we should go to them individually, then with witnesses, and finally take it to the church family. If they still refuse to see their offense, we are free to shake the dust from our feet and walk away from the relationship. Once an offending brother sees what he has done, however, we must not hesitate to show the same mercy to them that we have received from God and seek to appropriately restore the broken relationship.

This raises another very important question: What happens when our offending neighbor doesn't acknowledge their need for mercy? Should we wait until an offender acknowledges their shortcomings before we forgive them?

The answer is "no" – we don't need to wait until an offender takes responsibility for their actions before showing them mercy. If we did that, many of us would be trapped forever without the opportunity to be free from the pain of our wounds! I don't agree that an offender must acknowledge their responsibility for the wounds they have caused before we can show mercy, only that the wrong they have done must be acknowledged in front of them.

In the case of Valjean, for example, Valjean is not truly repentant until well after the bishop shows him mercy. But Valjean's sin is clearly exposed by the constable when he is caught red-handed with the bishop's silver. The crime is acknowledged and exposed for all to see. The constable sees it. The bishop sees it. Even Valjean sees it. And once the truth is laid on the table, mercy can finally do its work with the fullness of redemptive force.

Furthermore, there is some personal benefit to showing mercy to someone when they flat-out refuse to recognize their offense. For example, if I forgive someone for gossiping about me and doing harm to my reputation – even though she might not see herself in the wrong. In doing so, I set myself free from bitterness and anxiety that might keep me up at night. In that sense, showing mercy to someone who refuses to acknowledge their sin sets *me* free – even though it may do nothing for *them.* There is indeed some value in that.

Furthermore, the mere act of showing mercy to a pre-repentant brother *may actually prompt him to see the error of his ways.* This is another argument in favor of showing mercy before an offense is acknowledged by the offending party.

However, we should remember that this kind of mercy is usually for our own personal benefit, and unless the offense is sincerely acknowledged by the offender at some point, mercy may have very little of its intended, redemptive effect on them.

Regardless of the nuances of mistimed mercy, it is vitally important that offenses are first acknowledged in some form – if not by the offender themselves, than by society, family, or, at a minimum, face to face between the person who has been wronged and the person who has done the wrong.

Marionette Mercy

The second kind of false mercy is the kind that comes with strings attached. As long as even one condition for forgiveness remains in force after mercy has been given, that mercy is a fraud.

Human love is "iffy." It says, *"If you do XYZ,* I will show mercy." But this is not how our Heavenly Father is merciful – and nothing like the mercy of Holy Love as modeled by Jesus. Holy Love – the source of genuine mercy – is utterly without precondition.

Conditions are for contracts; they have no place in the sacred space of divine mercy and Holy Love. Bona fide mercy doesn't need to negotiate; it is confident enough in itself that it doesn't need anything from the offending person in order to feel secure. A system of *quid pro quo* belies true mercy.

Genuine mercy is remarkable **because** it waives the prerequisites human love normally requires. Human love says to a neighbor, "I will forgive you **as long as** you don't do it again." In contrast, Holy Love says, "I forgive you, **period.**"

The difference between the two is cosmic. Human love – mercy with strings attached – is in a vulnerable position because it **needs something** from the offending party. In contrast, Holy Love – mercy with no conditions – is in the strongest possible position because it **needs nothing** from the offender at all.

Human love is always insecure, and therefore feels the need to negotiate mercy. Holy Love, however, is secure in every way, and needs no tradeoff or conditions for forgiveness in order to feel complete or whole.

On a more practical note, when we attach strings to mercy we are essentially handing our neighbor control over our own joy. Strings attached at both ends. Our neighbor has the ability to drag us wherever they want when we rope them with conditional mercy.

We may think conditional mercy gives us the upper hand in a relationship, but it usually works the other way around. If my reactions are based on another person's actions, I am in their control. I am not free if my joy is tethered to the behavior of another human being. They own me.

Indeed, conditional mercy just gives my neighbor more buttons to push. Instead of controlling the relationship as I had hoped, I have merely weaponized it. Instead of restraining my neighbor, I have armed them. Conditional mercy gives my neighbor the opportunity to play me like a marionette.

True mercy cuts the strings, removing the conditions that allow us to be manipulated by our neighbor. May we have the courage to find our ultimate security as children of God, and not in our perceived control of others. Then we shall be free indeed!

Memorialized Mercy

Finally, true mercy keeps no record of wrongs. While false mercy keeps a running tab of every wayward glance and each harmful word, genuine mercy is able to forgive and forget. Holy Love knows how to move on.

Human love, for all of its frailty, has an immense capacity for remembering the wrongs others have done. We might agree to bury the hatchet with our neighbor, but we usually give it a shallow grave, put an X on the map, and keep a shovel handy so we can dig it up at a moment's notice. It is human nature to remember the past and hold prior offences over those we are supposed to love.

Like keepers of a grotesque formaldehyde menagerie, we cling to each and every wrong that has been done to us, eager to pull specimens off the shelf and admire our old wounds, prodding our brothers into despair over past shames. This is the counterfeit mercy of human love that wallows in the past.

But the mercy of Holy Love is different. According to the Scriptures, God actually "forgets" the past. (See Micah 7.19) Imagine that – one of Holy Love's defining characteristics is that it is *forgetful!*

Now, I don't imagine God is forgetful when it comes to names and faces, but when it comes to our past shortcomings He professes to be at a total loss.

"God, do you remember when I said that stupid, awful thing to my neighbor?"

"Hmm. Nope!"

"How about that time I *really* let my family down?"

"Sorry. Doesn't ring a bell."

"What about …"

"I'm sorry, I do not recall."

True mercy is secure enough to let go of the past. We don't need that dead weight holding us back. And neither do our neighbors need us to pull them down with the anchor of shame over their past indiscretions.

Authentic mercy cuts the anchor line and leaves the past on the ocean floor, setting us and our neighbor free to sail once again on the high seas of Holy Love.

"Forget the former things; do not dwell on the past. See, I am doing a new thing! Now it springs up; do you not perceive it? I am making a way in the wilderness and streams in the wasteland."

(Isaiah 43.18-19)

Mercy's Redemption

Jesus makes easy the answer to the question, "How far should I take mercy?" According to Him, we should stop showing mercy to others **at the exact point** where we would like God to stop showing mercy to us. Wherever we cut others off is where He will cut us off. As Jesus, the great Mercy Offering Himself, said:

"For in the same way you judge others, you will be judged, and with the measure you use, it will be measured to you." (Matthew 7.2)

And again:

"But if you do not forgive others their sins, your Father will not forgive your sins." (Matthew 6.15)

In the wrong context, mercy is debilitating and cheap… flirting with hypocrisy. In the right context, mercy is life-changing and sacred… approaching Holy. For those of us who believe in a better way – the way of Holy Love – there is no room for charades or counterfeits.

Fortunately, the author of Holy Love, the origin of mercy, is merciful even when we find ourselves to be frauds.

At this moment, we only see in part – in human love – with mercy that is shaded and blurred.

Then, however, we shall know mercy in full, just as we are fully known by Holy Love even now.

A Benediction
for Holy Love

Now may the true author of Holy Love
Embrace you with arms
Everlasting –
Everstrong –
Everstretched.
May He reach inside
To the corners of your heart that are as cold as stone
And raise you to life.

May He renew you with the breath of His Spirit
So that you might love Him
With all your heart,
With all your soul,
With all your strength.

And may you always love your neighbor
Better than you love yourself
Without harm
In constant service
And always overflowing with lifegiving mercy.
According to the heart of the Father,
And the soul of the Son,
And the strength of the Holy Spirit.

Amen

ABOUT THE AUTHOR

Steve Babbitt is Senior Pastor at Spring Valley Community Church in San Diego – a church he, his wife Tammie, and a handful of very brave friends planted in a park in 2003. The church is small in size but colossal in heart – you're invited to visit any Sunday morning for conversation and encouragement.

Steve earned an undergraduate degree in Journalism from Point Loma Nazarene University in 1995, and a Master's degree in Biblical Studies from Bethel Seminary San Diego in 2003. His work has appeared in numerous publications over the years, including USA Today, in the Associated Press, and dozens of various trade and local publications. A writer at heart, transcripts of Steve's sermons can be found on his church's website at svchurch.org.

Steve's wife, Tammie, is a seasoned educator and principal of a public elementary school. They have three remarkable children – an ambitious and beautiful daughter, and two compassionate and charming sons. **Each one** is soaring through life with flying colors!

Made in the USA
Columbia, SC
24 June 2019